I0456472

# I'm Not Dead… Yet

## How I Turned My Misfortunes Into Strengths

Dr. Joshua J. Caraballo

# © Copyright 2024 - All rights reserved.

The content contained within this book may not be reproduced, duplicated or transmitted without direct written permission from the author or the publisher.

Under no circumstances will any blame or legal responsibility be held against the publisher, or author, for any damages, reparation, or monetary loss due to the information contained within this book, either directly or indirectly.

Legal Notice:

This book is copyright protected. It is only for personal use. You cannot amend, distribute, sell, use, quote or paraphrase any part, or the content within this book, without the consent of the author or publisher.

Disclaimer Notice:

Please note the information contained within this document is for educational and entertainment purposes only. All effort has been executed to present accurate, up to date, reliable, complete information. No warranties of any kind are declared or implied. Readers acknowledge that the author is not engaged in the rendering of legal, financial, medical or professional advice. The content within this book has been derived from various sources. Please consult a licensed professional before attempting any techniques outlined in this book.

By reading this document, the reader agrees that under no circumstances is the author responsible for any losses, direct or indirect, that are incurred as a result of the use of the information contained within this document, including, but not limited to, errors, omissions, or inaccuracies.

# Table of Contents

# Dedication

This book is dedicated to anyone who has ever struggled and felt they don't belong in this world. Your misfortunes can turn into strengths if you want them to, and we all have the opportunity to stand on the shoulders of giants who have done it before us. Thank you to my parents, my brother, extended family, and my loving partner. You all have shown me what true love looks like, and your support has made me who I am today, and for that I am truly grateful.

# Introduction

Much is known of human life. Thanks to the dedicated work of people with many degrees to their name, we understand the behavior of the human body down to the very cells that make up our physical forms. However, for all the knowledge we have of the physical, so much has yet to be discovered of those aspects of human life that are decidedly less tangible. The effects of time on a human life is one such area that warrants further study. The longer we live, the more we know and the richer our wealth of experience to draw from. While our life experience is nothing if not useful, it can be an incredibly heavy weight to carry around with you. The past cannot be undone.

As onerous as the task of carrying around your past may sometimes be, it's worth considering that each memory that burdens us in this way is, in fact, a piece of the puzzle that fully comprises who we are. When we put them together, the jigsaw of our being is complete, and we can see the truth of who we are. Whether we understand that truth is another matter entirely, one that could be discussed at length by minds much more enlightened and philosophical than my own. Regardless, looking back on our lives is important, however old one may be. It is through this same retrospection that you and I meet each other here today.

The way in which a person looks back will depend on who they are, where they come from, and the person they have grown to be. As I engage in this retrospection, I see a life characterized by several milestone events, many of which followed the progression typical of human life. However, along with these milestones, there were others that were just as crucial to the formation of my personhood, and which I would dare say are not typical of everyone's lived experience. Over the course of the first few decades of my life, I experienced cancer, addiction, a number of mental health issues, and even spent some time in prison. In this period, there were stretches of time in which I felt disconnected from myself, from my heritage, and from my identity, which itself is so greatly informed by my background. And yet, here I am today, welcoming you to this book, eager to share the story of my life with you. In fact, that is exactly the purpose of this book. I hope that, in taking you through my past and all of its facets, you can unlock the powerful skills of perseverance, change, and self-acceptance that may lie dormant within you. I hope to help you gain these specific skills, as they are the very ones that got me through all the lowest moments of my life, and which ensured that I made it to the present.

This book is a narrative journey through my life, but only in part. In addition to telling this story, my goal is to meditate on the meaning of family, religion, love, and life. Ultimately, what this book hopes to become is a tool that you can use. Everything I have experienced in my life has taught me something. If all goes to plan, you can use the stories of similar experiences as a sort of guide to refer back to, and to steer you away from the same darkness I was in for so long. And while I can't promise that the story of my life will eradicate all the pain and suffering from yours, you may walk away from this book feeling slightly less alone in your struggles. With any luck, this sense of newfound connection will be accompanied by a shift in perspective.

Rest assured that I'm not trying to convince you of anything, nor attempting to use the pages of this book to convert you into one thing or another. What I am trying to do is to reflect on some of the things I've learned in my time on Earth. In the process, it's my hope that I may gain more insight into the human condition as it exists, develops, and evolves within the microcosm of society. And if all else fails, this book will serve to immortalize one person's experience and to preserve it for those who will follow. Who knows? Twenty years from now, a young, queer Puerto Rican kid might want some answer to their questions of identity, culture, belonging, and life, and they'll find this book. With luck, each of those answers will lie within the pages of this book, ready and waiting for their discovery. For those whose identities diverge somewhat from my own, I hope that you will undergo a similar learning process, if only to put the challenges you have faced from your own life into perspective. More importantly, it is my hope that, regardless of your identity, you will find something in my story that will help you take control and write the next chapter of your own story.

# Chapter 1:

# Entering the World—
# Naked and Unafraid

Decades ago, the calendar page turned, and the year became 1977. James "Jimmy" Carter was sworn in as the 39th president of the United States, the world was introduced to the Force when the first *Star Wars* film hit theaters, Miami experienced its first—and thus far only—snowstorm, and the country took a few steps in the name of progress, with the people of San Francisco electing openly gay politician Harvey Milk to the office of City Supervisor. And yet, as much as 1977 appears to have been a year of largely positive historical landmarks, things were far from ideal.

More specifically, in the 1970s, the further away the color of your skin and the practices of your culture were from White, the worse things were for you. Driving the attitudes of the 20th-century society even further home was the knowledge that things would be even less ideal if you were a person of color who fell under the rainbow umbrella of the LGBTQIA+ community. In fact, just a year after I was born, de Boer (1978) would write that "[h]uman rights, legitimately claimed by everybody, are withheld from homosexuals in our society." Like so many of the experiences that populate my life, describing queer people in such a clinical manner is very much a product of its time. The same can be said for a much longer list of words that someone from my background will have heard in the latter half of the 20th century.

Staying with the theme of race and ethnicity for a moment, it's worth mentioning that the experience of the Puerto Rican people, heterosexual or otherwise, wasn't exactly wonderful. After enduring insurrections in the 1950s and the rapid expansion of industry in the 1960s, many Puerto Ricans began the decade of the '70s living in slums in the Martín Peña canal, where they had been displaced after experiencing two horrific hurricanes (Kruhly, 2012). Even those who came over to the US in hopes of building a better life were faced with difficulties, this time in the form of racial discrimination, poverty, limited opportunities, and systemic oppression at its most potent. All of this to say that when I, a gay man of Puerto Rican descent, entered the world in 1977, the odds were very much stacked against me.

# A Beautifully Painful Experience on April 30, 1977

Childbirth is a strange thing. After nine long months of changes, ups and downs, worries, fears, preparation, and self-assurance, pain starts to kick in and a person changes from an adult to a parent. Stranger still is the perception we hold of the process. For those who aren't propped up by stirrups, experiencing pain that would put any stubbed toe to shame, childbirth is a time of frustration, fear (again), pain, and exhaustion. For those watching the events unfold from the safety of their position as designated supporter and hand-holder, childbirth is a glorious miracle—albeit one that involves more viscous components than you'd think. And then there's a third perspective still—one of blissful ignorance taken on by the one who is welcomed into the world, kicking, screaming, naked, and for the time being, unafraid. This three-pronged experience marked the beginning of my life on Saturday, April 30, 1977, at 06:56 p.m. As the world was quickly moving through the latter half of the decade, I drew my very first breath at Saint Vincent's Medical Center of Richmond in Staten Island, New York. And while some people were awaiting the relief they thought would come in the 1980s, I lay swaddled in my parents' arms, gleefully oblivious to what was yet to come.

There's something strange about trying to explain the process of childbirth from a nonclinical point of view. I think this is especially true for those of us who won't have that experience ourselves but will most likely participate in it from an external perspective. In looking at it in this way, I can't help but feel that there's a strange sense of futility to the whole thing. Not to start dipping my toe into nihilism so early on, but what other purpose is handed down to us from the moment we are born, other than to stay alive? And even that comes to an end. I sometimes think of it as a sadistic punchline to the cosmos' oldest, and worst, joke. We are born to live, and what is life without pain and suffering, without death? Without the latter, how would we even know anything or anyone is alive at all? And yet, through the mists of this doom-oriented thinking, I can still see the appeal in childbirth, and in all that follows. It must be glorious, that moment when you can inhabit the shoes of God (if you are of the religious persuasion), giving birth to a human, becoming a mighty creator yourself. And when the child has arrived, you have borne witness to a miracle, and the next years of your life will be filled with times in which you can give your offspring all the wonderful, happy experiences you have had. Still, my concern about that paradox remains: Some of the most wonderful things in life are achieved through pain. That is, I suppose, the fate of all those who succumb to the human condition. After all, without death, how would we know life? Without suffering, how would we know happiness? And without any pain, how would we grow or become better versions of ourselves?

By all accounts, my arrival in this world was a near-perfect example of this dichotomy of agony and elation. I weighed 7 pounds, 11 ounces, at birth, a size far too large for my mother, who stands at 4'10", if I were to make a generous estimate. In fact, as happy an occasion as this was, that day in 1977 would be the opening salvo of a lifelong struggle with pain and suffering, not only for me but for those around me as well. It should come as no surprise that my mother, waif of a woman that she is, struggled during delivery. Given our comparative sizes, labor was particularly difficult, and she left the delivery room having burst several of the blood vessels in her face due to the strain of the birthing process. Further physical damage came when it transpired that I had grown too large for her womb, causing my lower limbs to contort themselves so that my still-developing fetal body could be accommodated in utero. The pain of this occurrence would later evolve into discomfort, when my legs and feet were encased in plaster casts around my third month. Consequently, physical therapy was administered in the form of specialized shoes connected by a bar and worn at night in an attempt to realign my extremities into their typical form. Over the years, I've wondered if this was the first sacrifice my mother made for my sake. I've wondered if the bursting of the blood vessels was a means of creating space somewhere in her body, of taking away some of the pressure my exit through the birth canal was causing. I've wondered if part of her hoped that she could somehow make herself bigger in that moment, stretch her physical form in some way so that the agony would pass. I doubt it was her agony she was focused on, as pain is what many people accept their fate to be when it comes to childbirth. Perhaps this was the first demonstration of familial loyalty and love: My tiny mother earnestly trying anything she could to ease the pain she felt her newborn experiencing, even if this meant damaging parts of herself in the process.

I believe the moment of my birth to have set the tone for my life. In part, yes, it was the first instance among many of pain and discomfort, but it was also so much more than that. It was a moment in which the entirety of my life could have been defined, for better or worse. Coming out of the womb with my limbs entangled and in need of medical assistance could have meant that my life would be very different from what it became. Part of me still believes that this was some sort of test meant to determine whether I could handle the onus of living. I'm not entirely sure who administered this test, nor who analyzed and interpreted its results, but I believe it, nonetheless. Maybe my continued stubborn maintenance of this notion is a byproduct of my religious upbringing, the last vestiges of the parts of my mind that still engage in some measure of deification. Alternatively, it could simply be my way of conforming to the oldest of aspects of the human condition: I want to feel as though my presence here means something, as though I've earned my place in the cosmos. Whatever the true reason for this belief, the story of my birth—and all it entails—makes me feel vindicated in my argument for the concept of the suffering-happiness dichotomy. It's still early days, and we have much to cover before we reach the end of our journey. With that in mind, I have for you some comedic relief to end this rather heavy introductory section. After birth, the doctor slapped me on the bottom, as gynecological medics in the '70s were wont to do. In an act of what could be considered rebellion and righteous indignation, I proceeded to drench him in urine. In all likelihood, this expulsion was brought about by the physical stimulation of the slap. Whatever the cause, be it an instinctive reaction or the very first attempt at differentiation, in that moment, I was naked and unafraid.

# The Freedom of Not Choosing Your Family

So, by the time April 1977 came to a close, my first breath had been drawn, and I was officially a member of the human population. Naturally, I can't recall what my thoughts were in the time following my birth, if there were any thoughts present at all. However, I'd like to believe that my mental faculties were put to use to revel in my newfound freedom. I was no longer tethered to my mother's body, feeding from her, reliant on another person's maintenance of homeostasis to ensure my survival. More importantly, I was free from the cramped space of the womb, able to stretch and move as much as I'd like—well, as much as the mobility and physicality of a newborn baby allow. And yet, despite my hope that this was the gist of my internal monologue, I'm rather certain that the idea of freedom my little heart held didn't stretch beyond my imagination into practicality. This type of contradiction, this fundamental disconnect between what I'd like to see in the world (and what I'd like to believe it to be) and the reality of its state would come to be a theme in my life, the first instance of which took place the moment I was born. You see, where I thought I had traded the confines of the womb for the openness and freedom of the world, what had actually transpired was a transfer, as opposed to an exchange. For a moment, the edges of my world seemed infinite, then providence intervened, and walls were built with alarming speed.

Once again, we steer this narrative through the realms of reality and poetic license in equal measure. As an aside, I'd like to think of it as poetic license, but I am neither a poet, nor indeed an authority, in determining where the line between wishful thinking and embellishment lies. So, though everything in this book is patently true, I'd ask that you allow me my indulgence in descriptors, if only for the sake of coloring in what would otherwise be very bland proselytizing.

With that smooth segue locked into place, we move on to the matter of what those walls that were built upon my birth were, and how their existence felt very much like the universe sending me a message. This divine correspondence came in the form of my parents' religious practice. They were Jehovah's Witnesses, and because of the way these things tend to work, this meant that I was, too. I won't go into the details of what this religious practice entails, as this is neither the forum for that, nor are my experiences relevant to this particular part of the story.

In the years since childhood, when I have known periods of great freedom and great limitation, I wonder if some force greater than myself was trying to establish some sort of preventative measure. I wonder if this entity perhaps knew the path I would walk, and thus made an attempt to ensconce me within a community that was possibly as far removed from illicit behaviors as could be. However, how the decision was made to use the encampment of religion, I'll never understand. I think the aforementioned universal message may have been, "Don't make bad decisions," though my vanity wants it to be more profound. Nevertheless, there I was, a Jehovah's Witness since my first breath, tied to the values and beliefs of the adults around me.

I feel it imperative to mention that I hold very little resentment regarding my religious upbringing. My endless rumination of this part of my life comes from the fact that I can't seem to let go of my ideas about freedom and how little of it seems to be available to us readily and freely. What is important to note is that the institution of the Jehovah's Witnesses is found on conservatism. In the US, we tend to conflate conservatism in one aspect of life with conservatism across the entire spectrum of the human experience. As such, I should mention that I am wholly apolitical, as dictated by religious texts studied by zealots. So, while you couldn't accuse my family of being Republicans, the conservative label certainly applied to morality, sociality, and the way in which the world at large was regarded from within the confines of our little family unit. If you haven't yet realized why this belief system would prove to be problematic, allow me to remind you that the foundational aspects of my identity form part of what the religion regards as sinful. Not only would the very essence of who I am be deemed as wrong, but my actions would be filed under the category of "serious sins." Ergo, my sinning was on an entirely different level from those around me. There's an odd sense of pride I feel when thinking of this, if only to feel some sort of vindication. It's strange, I'm aware, but I believe in taking your wins where you can find them.

Neither my parents nor I could have known just how at odds my identity would be with the teachings of their scriptures and religious officials. Obviously, I can't say that, had we been in possession of that knowledge, things would have turned out differently. I didn't have the freedom to choose, so a choice was made on my behalf. As much as I would love to feel some sort of righteous indignation about this, I can't help but think of the ways in which my parents were raised and wonder if they had the freedom they imagined they did.

Did my grandparents? Did my great-grandparents? It seems to me that freedom exists, and it can be exercised, but only in matters that concern the smaller things in life. In those instances when we make big, life-altering decisions, freedom becomes something else. It's not entirely an illusion, nor is it as pure or as personal as we'd like to believe. Instead, the freedom we use to make choices is one move influenced by millions made before it. All we do is the result of all that has been done—for better, and perhaps God knows, for worse.

## The Man of House

Nearly three decades before my introduction to the human world, my father entered this life in 1940s New York City. The baby born in 1949 would go on to have a life characterized by experiences that, for lack of a better description, made for very compelling stories during my childhood. In his youth, my father was no stranger to difficulty. Before enlisting in the military, he was a member of a New York gang, made use of recreational drugs, and engaged in acts of violence. Though I can't credibly claim to understand the intricate working of human genetics, there is a strong case to be made for a genetic component of addiction. So, who knows? Maybe my father's stories should have been a hint (or a warning) for what was to come. To a degree, this would make sense. My father was a staunch traditionalist when it came to masculinity—at least when I was a child. During childhood, both my brother and I were provided with a very specific example of manhood, one that my father inhabited as a means of keeping the wheels of his conventional system turning. The problem is, these wheels may turn, but they are surprisingly ineffectual at generating any sort of movement. At times, something might move one way, but for as long as they remain in the same formation, their direction will always go unchanged.

Later on, my father joined the armed forces, serving as part of the airborne division. During his years as part of the troops, my father saw the light of God when he met with members of the Jehovah's Witnesses, who introduced him to the core tenets of their religious practice. Throughout his life, little had been consistent, and his conversion was an attempt at finding the thing that had always eluded him, something concrete and lasting. My father found was he was looking for, settling comfortably within the structure of the Jehovah's Witness religion, and finding the sense of purpose he'd been lacking until then. Finding religion was truly my father's saving grace, changing him on a fundamental level. His devotion to his newfound faith ran so deep that he would report for his daily military duties, Holy Bible in hand. After an eventful three years full of salvation and reinvention, my father was honorably discharged, and his time in the military came to an end.

Despite all this, the regimentation and rigor of the army stayed with him. So, when the time came to settle down and start a family, the strictness of his experience was naturally transferred into his family life. Once he assumed the role of father, he became the house disciplinarian, and this role meant that he set the tone for the family when it came to acceptable behaviors and beliefs. My father's faith was an incredibly important component of his life, so naturally, it became a prominent fixture in the rest of our lives, as well. With the benefit of hindsight and maturity, I can more fully understand the thought process behind raising me and my siblings using such a strict, religion-oriented parental style. To my father, Jehovah and his congregants were the greatest source of happiness, security, and salvation. Believing in my father's god meant that we would be kept safe in the same way he believed himself to be. By being adamant about studying the Christian Bible, my father felt that he was keeping us safe and allowing us access to something beyond ourselves. Knowing how fiercely he clung to his beliefs, and how much they contributed to changing his life, I can see now that he created this specific domestic atmosphere as a means of sharing with us the core part of who he was. Religion permeated everything in our household. Rites of worship and attending Kingdom Hall were regular fixtures of our daily and weekly schedules. Life was lived around the religion and its teachings, and every action was to be carried out in exaltation of God with the utmost reverence for his might.

Our family dynamics were constructed according to the biblical designation of the man as the head of the home. Listening to my father was the recommended course of action—actually, it was more required than recommended. He took his paternal role very seriously and was very particular about what he expected from his wife and children. It will come as no surprise that my father was a traditionalist. In the 1970s and '80s, for all the progress being made by second-wave feminism, a reliance on gendered domestic roles supposedly made America strong, and would ensure that my father raised good, hardworking, respectful children. It must be said that his having this perspective wasn't entirely negative, as it meant that he was involved in our lives to a considerable degree. Regrettably, this single sentence is where the silver lining begins and ends. My father's adherence to conservative traditionalism resulted in the perpetuation of a toxic cycle of masculine ideals, power dynamics, and blind family loyalty. To my father's mind, his role as head of the household meant that he was to be the breadwinner, the disciplinarian, the protector, and a myriad of other things that meant he could become what he regarded as the truest type of man.

Unfortunately, my father's methods didn't involve only his actions or attitudes. In pursuit of becoming a real man, my father ensured that my mother was subservient, that she was humble, and that she understood her role in the household to be inferior to his. As far as he was concerned, she was a supplemental aid to his attempts to maintain control of the family. A memorable instance of his strict adherence to the values of loyalty and respect for pre-established dynamics involves a trip to see my grandfather. Their relationship was far from ideal, with my grandfather having been abusive toward my dad, as a child, on many occasions. One example among many that demonstrate the severity of his actions includes forcing my father to kneel upon a pile of uncooked rice, from which he wasn't allowed to move until blood had been drawn from his legs. This brutality formed a part of the image

I had of my grandfather. The rest of the picture was configured during our visits, which weren't infrequent. By the time I arrived and was old enough to recall seeing my grandfather, decades of smoking had taken its toll on him, leading to the development of emphysema. My memories of our days with him are largely indiscernible and involve him being confined to a chair largely immobile. He would sit there with an oxygen tank resting next to his chair, a tube leading up from it to a mask strapped to his face. Occasionally, the hiss of his breathing from the tank's supply would be interrupted when he took the mask off, either saying something in Spanish or otherwise putting his breathing on hold to take a drag from a cigarette.

One day, our visit was cut short when my grandfather took the mask off once more, again to say something in Spanish. This time, it was an expletive—*puta*—directed at my mother. One of the less elegant Spanish words, *puta* translates to "whore" in English. Naturally, my mother felt unsettled by this, and our departure came soon after, as she became overwhelmed with emotion. Unfortunately, the day didn't end there. As we drove home, my father (ever the familial loyalist) informed us all that we would be returning the following week to see our grandfather again. Though I can't recall the exact expression that passed across my mother's face, I remember that it was far from pleased. My father caught sight of this and proceeded to remind us that his father was, after all, a member of the family. We were told that family wasn't discarded, regardless of the nature of their treatment of you. Family, he informed us, were to be the recipients of our unconditional love.

No matter what was said or done, this love was to be expressed, and it was never to cease.

At the risk of appearing to make excuses for my father, I feel compelled to mention that I don't resent him for his chosen style of parenthood, or for his choice of religious practice. The further away I move from my own childhood, the clearer my comprehension of my father as a human being becomes. Like countless others across the globe, he was faced with an ultimatum when he first became a dad: Either he could choose to carve a new road on his journey through parenthood, eschewing his parents' practices, or he could rely on what he had seen, heard, and experience firsthand. His decision to follow the latter path was, I'm sure, influenced by his adoption of a socially restrictive religion. All he did was the result of all that had been done. All his parents did was the result of all that had been done in their youth, too. The cycle of parental emulation continued with him, and all I did was the result of all that had been done. The wheel spun once more.

# The *Real* Man of the House

For all my father's machismo and strictness, our household saw the same subtle shift in power that many others experienced across the world in the '70s and '80s. Female empowerment was young and still a ways away from functioning as an independent, practicable concept. Despite the fact that it was impossible for my mother to explicitly assume the role of domestic head, everyone in the house held the same sort of subtle understanding regarding the true dispersal of power within our parents' relationship. On the surface, my father was the highest of authorities, laying down the law, enforcing its recognition, and steering the family away from the perils of the world. However, one needed to look only inches below that same surface to be confronted with the reality—my mother was the *real* man of the house, in the way that mothers the world over sometimes are; authority started and ended with her. This particular subversion of traditional gender roles could not be overt, as it would stand in direct contradiction with the way in which my father believed men and women should interact, especially within the context of domestic living. And yet, my mother knew how to assert herself in ways that would allow him to retain his sense of control while simultaneously letting the rest of us know how things were truly operating.

One must understand that the power my mother wielded within our household wasn't easily gained, nor was holding on to it as effortless as it may sometimes have appeared. The older I become, the better I understand just how hard my mother worked at tipping the scales in her favor, and how carefully she had to operate in order to preserve the relative calm that came with my father's perception of the extent of his power. I'm hesitant to call my mother cunning, as I believe her actions to have been born out of great intelligence rather than malice, though I must concede that there was a measure of slyness to her maintenance of authority. Had we lived in an ideal world, her deft manipulation of interpersonal dynamics could have been a natural talent, one she used for greater things than keeping the inner workings of the family entity as close to homeostatic as possible.

Unfortunately, our world was far from ideal. My mother hails from Puerto Rico, born in 1951 in the city of Humacao, situated on the eastern coast of the island nation. Though her upbringing was typical of what one might expect of the 1950s and '60s, her family life was somewhat more complicated. Being one of eight siblings, things were already relatively atypical, despite the fact that large families were not so unusual at the time. The number of people in the house wasn't the only notable factor; rather, it was the fact that she was one of six sisters, with the total number of eight siblings being rounded out by two brothers. Among the children, there were four different fathers, making the branches of the family tree a bit more intertwined than one would expect. And yet, none of this can be designated as the cause of my mother's quiet fortitude, or indeed her impressive ability to subtly make her presence known.

The way in which my mother was able to consistently assert her power in our home came in part from the fact that she had to fight to be heard from among the noise of her seven siblings. However, even more crucial to the shaping of her personhood was the abuse she endured at the hand of her father. My mother had to fight to make it out, she had to fight to achieve some semblance of being okay, and she had to fight to hold on to the power that her past could so easily have robbed her of. She carried this fighting spirit into her marriage and stoked its flames as she transitioned into motherhood. While I'm certain that my mother loves my father, I'm also certain that she recognized the abuse he suffered from his father and knew the extent of the damage its aftermath could wreak on her own children. She knew that overt resistance would achieve nothing at all—or might risk making things worse. So, she worked in the quieter worlds of subtlety, nuance, and diplomacy, ensuring that the way her children thought of their home was light years removed from her own recollections.

Naturally, I wasn't aware of the reasons behind my mother's existence as the highest authority in the home, yet I nevertheless felt compelled to forge a deeper bond with her than with my father. This compulsion, and indeed the depth of my bond with my mother, wasn't born out of anger, nor out of a desire to reject my father's love or distance myself from him. Rather, I believe the closeness my mother and I shared came from the intensity of our experiences with pain, both individual and shared. The latter is perhaps the greatest reason of all and comes from the time of my birth, when both my body and hers were stretched, contorted, and handled in ways they were not meant to endure, much less withstand. After the trauma of this experience, my mother became fiercely protective of me, and I of her. I suppose that, on her part, this is typical of motherhood, with the lengths she went to in order to shield me from harm being only slightly more intense than those of other mothers. If this is the case, the intensity can once more be chalked up to the pain of that day in 1977. As for the sense of protection I felt for my mother, I suppose this can be traced to some sort of unconscious awareness of our shared trauma.

Perhaps I understood, even in my infancy and childhood, that my arrival in this world had harmed her in some way. Perhaps the creation of our bond was some form of penitence on my part. I could theorize all day, but I fear I won't ever find an answer that satisfies all possible avenues of origin.

Regardless of the reason for it, my mother and I were close. The responsibility she felt for me was reciprocated, and I believed the onus lay upon me to protect her just as much as she always protected me. I recall one instance in particular when I felt this sense of obligation very strongly. Years ago, my mother got her finger caught in a mouse trap when she reached her hand into a closet. I was standing behind her when this happened and was close enough to feel her scream reverberate through my body. Actually, as I look back on it now, I don't know that I could in actual fact feel the vibrations of her crying out. It seems to me now that the intensity of my emotional response spilled over into the realm of the physical, perhaps in an attempt by my brain to replicate the distress my mother was experiencing.

Physical or not, I remember being shook to my core when I heard her scream, so much so that I immediately began to weep. My tears weren't shed because of any fear I felt for my mother's experience of pain, but rather because I stood behind her, unable to do much–if anything–to make things better for her. Years later, this would still be my go-to response. Whenever I feel helpless or out of my depth, I feel myself start to well up. As I got older, this response would change slightly. Though tears were never that far behind when I encountered these situations, my reaction would sometimes veer in another direction, albeit one that was just about the same in terms of intensity. When I didn't cry in those moments, stubbornness set in, making me adamant that I would find and implement a solution, regardless of what it might take. It's funny, looking back on one's life like this, to see what makes the cut for profundity. In this case, no one was severely injured, but the experience still sticks with me all these years later. It just goes to show that the scale of an event does not always equate to the impact it has on a person, and that some of life's most valuable lessons can be learned in smaller, simpler moments.

## Sibling Rivalry

Completing the portrait of the family Caraballo are the stories of the trials and tribulations of the family's younger generation. As the title of this section suggests, it's time to take a look at that age-old tradition, one that renders any multi-offspring family incomplete until it has come to pass: the always fun, rarely traumatizing act of sibling rivalry. It's worth pointing out that my brother did not, in fact, traumatize me, but making dramatic statements like this comes with the territory of being the younger sibling.

I don't think my brother and I were destined to be close to each other, at least not in the first few years we spent together. Things between the two of us were less than ideal from the start, though truth be told, I understand why he felt some of the animosity he did. For seven long years, my brother was the only child, so you can imagine that he was less than thrilled when he learned he would be unseated as the youngest member of the family, and that he would have to become lumped in with me to form the newest level of branches along the family tree. However, I would learn later that my conception was motivated in large part by my brother's incessant requests for a younger brother.

Whatever friction there was between the two of us may have to be chalked up to the old adage of being careful what you wish for. My brother's perception of becoming an elder sibling was already tinged with negativity, then my mother brought me home from the hospital. Had my introduction to the household gone smoothly and had there been nothing of note to report from the delivery process, I believe things may have turned out different for my brother and me, if only slightly. Alas, this was not the case. Not only did my mother bring home my brother's usurper, but that very same child had caused damage to his mother. When he saw the physical toll my birth had taken, he felt there was only one person to blame. Along with condemning me as the one who caused this harm (the logic of which I can understand, especially when espoused by a seven-year-old), my brother saw my mother's injuries and swiftly decided that things would have been better had I not been born at all. From my perspective, this was more than just a decision; it was his wish.

I don't know how long my brother held on to this grudge, but I know that things wouldn't have been easy between us even without that initial assignation of blame. With nearly a decade of lived experience separating the two of us, our perspectives, thoughts, and overall dispositions would stand in near-total contradiction with each other at any given moment. Yet, despite how little he wanted me around his home and in his life, I couldn't help but look at him the same way all younger siblings look at those who came before them. I felt that, because I had caused so much trouble at the start of my life, the least I could do with the rest of it was to try to be the best child I could possibly be. Not only did this mean pleasing my parents and trying to live up to their standards, it also meant getting on my brother's good side. It won't come as a massive shock to you that the latter goal wasn't quite that manageable, at least not as easily as I'd hoped. You see, I idolized my older brother. To me, there was no one cooler than him, no personality or character more aspirational than him. I hung around him as much as I could, hoping that my attempts at emulation would eventually give way to an influx of traits, thoughts, and feelings that would make me just like him. Of course, having this goal also meant that I wanted to be my brother's closest friend, something I felt would be impossible to achieve for as long as I remained stuck in childhood, so far behind him as he made his way into adolescence while I was only just becoming a person in my own right.

Much of the reason I desired this level of closeness and identification with my brother stemmed from the happiness he appeared to experience so regularly, and so intensely. From my perspective as the runty little brother, he didn't have a care in the world. No restrictions, no doubts, no shame, nor any fear. You can imagine what this felt like to someone who was physically restricted for much of their childhood, and who could easily be reduced to tears when loved ones experienced pain or discomfort. To me, my brother's way of being was everything I needed to be. Despite how desperate I was to attain this type of happiness, and despite my hope that my brother would readily share the secrets to his emotionally untethered state, and that this would result in affection flowing both ways, there was a bit more competition for his attention than I'd anticipated.

There was a memorable instance early on in my life that significantly demonstrates just how profound the disconnect between us was. Our cousin from New York came to visit us, and during his stay, there was nothing I wanted more than to just spend time with the two of them. I suppose my goal with this was familiarization, but there was also a part of me that hoped I would pick up a thing or two about being, well, them. Predictably, they didn't share the same ideas regarding how their time together would be spent. In spite of my attempts to hang around them, they soon moved their activities outside. Naturally, I followed. As they walked around, my (very inconspicuous) pursuit continued. Eventually, they grew tired of having me as their little tail, and they took off running. Being nearly a decade younger, I couldn't keep up, and they left me in the dust. They were successful in losing me, and if I'm entirely honest, looking back, I don't think I had ever felt quite so lost.

I remember running home to my mother and declaring the truth of my disturbed state. Suffice to say that my brother got an earful when he came home. In hindsight, sharing the details of this particular experience with my mother did more harm than good. Though I long suspected that my brother didn't care for me all that much at the time, it was all but confirmed from that day forward. As much as I would love to feign indignation at this turn of events, I understand where my brother was coming from. He hadn't wanted my company, he'd made it clear, and yet he had gotten in trouble. In my mind, I had done the right thing by sharing the details with our mother, but he saw this differently. In the years to come, this would be a defining characteristic of our relationship.

Even in those rare instances in which we managed to do something together, things rarely went smoothly. To illustrate my point, I would like to share with you the fact that, every year on my parents' wedding anniversary, my gift to them was a play. Now, God-fearing Jehovah's Witnesses that we were, this play would be based on a scene from the Bible. One year, my creative process led me to stage a re-enactment of the death of Jezebel. If you are unaware, Jezebel was an Old Testament harlot (not my preferred term, but it'll do for accuracy's sake). She lived at the very top of a tower, which meant that, to provide accuracy, I was perched at the very top of my childhood home's staircase. As the story goes, the Lord sent one of his men on a quest, the end goal of which was to climb to the top of the tower, throw Jezebel from it, and allow her to be eaten by the dogs lying in wait at the foot of the structure. In our re-enactment, my brother and I had padded each stair as well as the bottom landing with pillows to ensure my fate wasn't similar to that of

Jezebel's. When the pivotal moment came, my brother elected to change from the previously agreed-upon push to a spur-of-the-moment shove. What followed was my careering through the air, missing most of the staircase, bypassing the pillows, and coming to rest on the floor, my temple cracked open by a porcelain cat. Needless to say, the performance came to a screeching halt as I was taken to the hospital to receive stitches.

In the same way that I often wonder how my relationship with my father could have been different, or why my relationship with my mother exists in the state it does, I regularly find myself considering the possibility that something larger was at play during those early years. As I learned to grow more sure of myself, cultivating my identity and making my peace with it, I increasingly believe envy to have been a mitigating factor. On my brother's part, he may have felt envious of the closeness I had with our mother. For me, however, the envy ran deeper. My brother's happiness in life was something I desperately wanted, but this desire extended beyond mere contentment with life, as I wanted the image I saw of myself to be just as clear and concrete as the one he held of himself. In addition to every other thing about him that was cool and out of my grasp, it was his confidence in who he was that really struck a chord. Though I'd only identify the true nature of it later on, I felt an incredible lack of tethering in those early years. I knew I was different, and I was already able to identify some of the areas where my life and identity diverged from that of the people around me. What I didn't know was how profound this difference truly was. All I knew was that

I was dissatisfied, that I was scared, and that, on some fundamental level, I was wrong.

# The Art of Being Sick

Any portrait of my early years would be incomplete without mentioning the fact that my life, for whatever reason, has almost always been linked to illness. We've already explored, in painstaking detail, the traumatizing physical effects my birth had on both me and my mother. Furthermore, we've already established that the earliest period of my life was dotted with doctor's visits, physical therapies, and other treatments. However, as important as it is to take note of my early association with the world of the clinician, it is equally imperative to understand that there was significant overlap between the life I lived in the halls of hospitals and the one I lived at home. Now, I was rather sickly as a child, at least to my recollection. I'm not saying that it's a competition, but I'm pretty sure I could have given just about any ailing Victorian child a run for their money. There's an odd feeling of pride I have as I write that sentence, the origins of which I'd like to avoid exploring, if it's all the same to you. My triumph over the frailty of 18th-century British children aside, illness was something I came to know very well. It seemed that no single year would pass without my contracting one sickness or another.

One year, memorably, whooping cough decided to set up shop in my respiratory system. My mother tried her best to keep me healthy and to nurse through my convalescence when I became ill. Always the pragmatist, she regularly gave me over-the-counter medication, both in an effort to combat whatever internal distress I was experiencing, and also in the hopes that it would stave off the next bout of illness—though we both understood that the latter was likely more an exercise in self-reassurance than anything else.

Unfortunately, my mother's efforts never quite seemed to take hold. Even when I wasn't diagnosable, I recall always being slightly ill. Now, I recognize this pattern of questionable health followed by more severe sickness as the sign of a weakened immune system. In the '80s, this wasn't known to us, and even if it had been, you can imagine that the resources held by a minority family weren't exactly expansive. So, sickness was another thing that became subsumed into my perception of what "normal" was, even though it was anything but.

My more optimistic side likes to think that this was a form of introduction to what my life would become, a sort of preparatory immunological exercise intended to signal how my future would play out. Being different from the other children, both in terms of physicality and personality, was something I accepted as being typical of my life. Little did I know that this first taste of deviation from the norm would come to overwhelm the palate of my life—a sort of umami foreshadowing, if you will. I knew what I thought was normal, and as most of us do, I knew little of anything else. What I *did* know was that those things that lay outside the norm (the one in which everyone is happy, healthy, and as close to the ideal masculine as possible) should be regarded as manifestations of some sort of sickness. While the symptoms would vary, with some being sick in their souls and others in their bodies alone, it was made explicitly clear to me that anything other than that norm was tantamount to hell.

## Forging an Identity at Odds

As the first stage of our journey, my early childhood, comes to a close, the final foundational brick comes slotted into place. It's imperative that this understanding exists first; otherwise, the rest of my life's story is likely to contain some gaps, subtextually speaking. This last brick is, in fact, one we've already touched upon: the contradiction of identity, and how it influences an individual's perception of the norm. Admittedly, this sounds like the title of a graduate student thesis, though, thankfully, only in theory. In reality, it's a far more disorienting experience, one that has the potential to turn your world upside down.

I understood that my upbringing was something of an exception to what many consider to be the societal rule, even in a time when religious practice influenced a greater deal of rules, conventions, and ideals. Being raised as a Jehovah's Witness meant being taught doctrines and being encouraged to adopt spiritual values that deviated from the beliefs being pontificated upon in mainstream Christian denominations. All this is to say that, given the heritable quality assigned to religion, my life was atypical from the moment it started. And yet, the fact that my family's beliefs differed from those of others in our community, or indeed of those of my friends, never perturbed me as a child. What we did in our home, we considered normal, and the same could be said for every other household on our block. Everyone had their own version of what was typical, and that was fine. You know, the normalcy, dryer settings, and all that.

I feel the need to stress the subjectivity of normality, particularly when it comes to individual choices, because I must confess the fact that my family's religious affiliations never bothered me much. In fact, I eagerly threw myself into the culture of the religion. I embraced the teachings, happily accepting that the celebration of birthdays, Christmas, and other holidays weren't meant for us. Instead, we were taught that this celebratory, thankful spirit was one we should carry with us every day. This logic is actually quite sound, as our parents would regularly remind us that we should always feel gratitude for life, not only on certain designated days. Naturally, this argument was applied to birthdays only. The Yuletide was something else entirely, and we were taught to eschew Christmas celebrations as they were pagan in nature and as such diametrically opposed to who and what we were as Jehovah's Witnesses. And yet, even in our adherence to this norm, my family managed to make the Jehovah's Witnesses' practices our own. While my parents were resolute in their refusal to acknowledge birthdays, they did make a point of celebrating their wedding anniversary. The act in itself is hardly radical, but it's the way in which they celebrated that sticks with me all these years later. Every year, on every anniversary, we would take part in the festive spirit by exchanging wrapped gifts. It was never said out loud, but we all understood this to be our own, private version of Christmas.

To many, giving and receiving gifts on an anniversary is unremarkable, and I'm sure you could argue that this small act of subversion didn't amount to much, given that we were still loyal, pious Witnesses. I'm sure that you'd be right to make this argument, or at the very least have a logical basis for it. However, it's important to remember that the goal was never to radicalize us, or to change how we saw the church and its teachings. The whole idea behind the anniversary gifts was to have a good time as a family, to come together and do something that was just ours. In the grand scheme of things, this did little to sway events one way or another, but in the context of my little life, these occasions made all the difference. They were the first of many instances in which the things I did, the things I thought, and the way I perceived myself to be stood at odds with one another. Throughout my life, contradictions like these would crop up time and time again in everything from how well (or, rather, how badly) I thought of myself, to the type of medical treatment I sought in adulthood, as well as generally informing my decision-making abilities. It's also worth noting that I have a very high tolerance for ambivalence, something I'm nearly entirely sure can be traced back to the many contradictory ideas and thoughts I dealt with during my formative years.

Of all the times I found myself possessing an identity at odds with itself (and with the world in which I lived), I don't think any had a more lasting impact on me than when the forging of that identity required the examination of my sexuality. The curriculum according to which my religious beliefs were dispensed taught us that there were do's and don'ts when it came to things like sex and love, and that the flexibility of these taboos was nonexistent. The list of things that were permissible was expansive and covered thoughts and behaviors related to all sexual identities. The heterosexual kids, for whom sex was allowed, were given strict parameters regarding their amorous endeavors. Sex was fine, as long as it was within the bounds of marriage. Sex with someone to whom you weren't married? No dice, regardless of your marital status. As for sex with someone whose pronouns were the same as yours, no allowances were made. It wasn't a matter of waiting until marriage; it was complete and total abstention.

When I was first introduced to these rules, they didn't affect me all that much. They were there to guide us, so I filed all the relevant information in the back of my mind and didn't think much more of it. At least, that was the intention. Worries, fears, and ruminations about sexuality would regularly situate themselves in my consciousness. As a child, this scared me, particularly because I couldn't find any logical reason for their appearance. As an adult, it's all too easy to see why I was so preoccupied with this particular issue. Fortunately (I think), the reason for these thoughts wouldn't remain secret for the entirety of my childhood. I remember the first time I realized that something within me had deviated from what was the norm back then. In true 20th-century style, this revelation descended upon me while I was flicking through a JCPenney catalog. I found myself drawn to the photos of the male models, and not in a way that would suggest the clothes were what fascinated me. I found myself undergoing the same rite of passage as queer boys the world over every time I found myself in the men's underwear section of the catalog. Each image that passed before my young eyes struck me with its beauty. I was still too far away from adolescence to attach the concept of sexual attraction to those photos, and yet I knew that the way in which my body and mind reacted to these sights was, at the same time, overwhelmingly visceral and entirely natural. In later years, this event would prove to be extremely influential. Though I didn't know it at the time, it formed one of the bricks I would use to build the foundational layer of my personhood. While certainly cemented into place with surprising strength, this brick would contribute more to destruction than anything else.

Chapter 2:

# Growing Pains—One-and-a-Half Dozen

As it tends to do, life wore on, and things changed as I made my way into the choppy waters of childhood and preadolescence. In the period of time covering these years, as well as those rose-colored days of adolescence, my life seemed to be a never-ending parade of surprises, changes, and discoveries.

## Mama's Boy

Anyone who has dabbled in even the smallest portion of child developmental psychology can tell you that one of the greatest sources from which kids extract their personalities and behaviors is their parents. In this field, the practice of "behavioral" modeling is often discussed. The name explains the concept relatively effectively, it being the way in which our actions as adults, parents, and caretakers imprint upon the very impressionable, very absorbent minds of young children. Much of who we are early on in life comes from what we see and what our parental figures do and say. Over time, our sense of self becomes more individualized, and we either move away from what our parents taught us or find ways to adapt them to suit us. Regardless, the bedrock is laid in those early, formative years, and its shape is steadily chiseled into existence by our caregivers.

If you are starting to question why child psychology concepts are being discussed in an autobiography, rest assured that I have a point, which is this: When I was a child, I saw what the adults in my life did, and because I loved and trusted them, I thought I should do it, too. Now, ideally, this would mean that I emulated their more positive—or more pious, depending on your point of view—attributes, and that things should have gone swimmingly. Had it been that way, I'd have a hell of a lot less to talk about in these pages. However, the attributes I chose to adopt from the people around me weren't regarded as the most ideal qualities for a young boy to assume. Instead of absorbing the machismo of the men around me, I opted to spend time with the women and girls of the family. I felt this innate sense of attraction to them, separate from the feelings that the catalogs elicited, yet just as potent.

There are no specific attributes or demeanors I can pinpoint as the catalyst for my desire to spend time with the opposite sex. It was just a general sort of desire to be what they were, to be how they were. I felt comfortable in their presence. It was as though the façade I was so painstakingly working to construct simply melted away. In its place was constructed something entirely different, something far more natural, in which I felt like myself, comfortable and secure. It must be said, though, that I didn't understand this was happening. From my perspective, I was easing into a new space, one in which I felt safe, especially when I was able to more closely mimic the behaviors and mannerisms of my mother, aunt, and the other women I spent time with. I wasn't aware that I was deviating from some masculine norm, or indeed that the version of masculinity I showed the world was inaccurate—at least, as it pertained to my true sense of self.

This attraction—for want of a better, more precise term—began shortly after we left New York and settled in Florida. Now living on a new stretch of coast, we made our home with one of my maternal aunts. Though the adjustment took some time, everything appeared to be relatively smooth sailing. But, as most things in the formative years do, something went awry. The comfort I felt in becoming more like the women I knew was, sadly, a feeling restricted only to myself. To the men in my life, it seemed that I was doing something wrong, something I had no business doing. In one memorable instance, my dad chastised me for standing in what he deemed to be an unbecoming, feminine position. Years later, I would learn that this particular stance was innocuous enough, belonging to the world of yoga, and not that of any particular sex. The pose in question had me assuming a position similar to that of a flamingo. You likely have seen it. It's the one where you stand on one leg, lifting the other foot so that it rests against the thigh of the leg planted on the floor. To this day, I'm not sure where I picked it up, or indeed how standing in this way is connected to elevated femininity.

Nevertheless, I was made to see the error of my ways, receiving feedback from people in every part of my life. Their advice, opinions, and convictions would be shared, regardless of whether it had been solicited. My father's contribution to this chorus relied heavily on the same sentiments I had been hearing for some time. I was told that my posture (the one taken from an ancient yogic practice) was wrong, overly feminine, and something that I should avoid. What my father said confused me. To me, it made no sense to care about the way in which another person stood. This confusion was only deepened every time the feedback was given again, which believe me, was often enough to make an impression. When I sat down, I would cross my legs, and again I was alerted of a mistake. These were things that were shared with me time and time again, at home, at Jehovah's Witness meetings, and at school. In the case of the latter, people took notice of the fact that the particular way in which boyhood had manifested within me differed somewhat from the versions possessed by my classmates.

I now attribute much of my comfort emulating the women in my life to the closeness I held with my mother, especially during my childhood. My sexuality is sure to have played a role, given that the very essence of who I am was a deviation from what was regarded as typical for the time. However, it was because my mother was the one who comforted, protected, and supported me that I sought to be like her. Perhaps I understood that doing this meant that I was creating an authentic identity for the first time. Perhaps I just enjoyed feeling like I belonged among the women, a sensation that eluded me in the presence of my father and brother. Whatever the exact cause for my emulation, the bond between mother and son is sure to have played a significant role.

I feel that we've reached an important juncture at which I must explain that my desire to act in a more traditionally feminine way (*effeminate*, as some pedants would say) is in no way meant to indicate that I somehow wanted to be a woman. Forgive me for the lecturing tone, but this is a distinction that needs to be made, as the two are often conflated. One's sexuality is not their gender, and vice versa. I have always felt sure of the fact that I am a man, that the way in which I present myself to the world aligns with the gender marker noted on my birth certificate. I'm lucky that way. I recount this particular event in my life to illustrate that finding my place in the world involved carving out a form of masculine presentation and perception that worked for me.

When I was a child, I believed this to be what I learned from the women I surrounded myself with. When I was subsequently disabused of this notion, the onus fell upon me to find some sort of middle ground, and to determine how I would see myself when it came to being a man. This was the realization I came back to at the time. It could just as easily have been another revelation entirely, and I would be telling you a very different story. This was not the case for me, though it certainly was for others. I'll stop the rambling here, simply saying that being confronted with what a man was "meant" to be led to a re-evaluation of one part of myself. For others of my generation, being forced into boxes like these had wider-ranging effects. Whatever the outcome, all of us were made to feel awkward, different, or wrong somehow. It's an unfortunate truth, but the truth, nonetheless.

Trust me when I say that revelations such as these are profoundly striking to me as an adult. Now, with the benefit of hindsight and a few experiential notches on my belt, I understand the nature of my childhood much better. However, suffice it to say this was not the case in the final decades of the 20th century. Now, I understand that what I endured as a child, particularly as it pertained to my mannerisms, were born out of fear, misogyny, and other similar unpleasant behavioral traits. The problem is, we didn't have the words to describe these phenomena, at least not in my neck of the woods. Back then, there was what was done and what wasn't. Everything that fell into the latter category was in need of repairing, so that was what I tried to do. I put every bit of effort I could muster into "correcting" myself, to stop the leg-crossing and hip-tilting, to turn myself into the developing young man I was meant or supposed to be. Regrettably (or maybe not), my labors proved to be unfruitful. I failed. A lot. The result was a lot of self-doubt and self-hatred, accompanied by a lot of bullying, as well as a singular schoolyard beating.

## Getting Closer to the Equator

Realigning myself with these societal norms and standards was a difficult thing to achieve, and I'm not entirely sure that I ever really succeeded (perhaps thankfully). The trouble is, difficulty and hardship are very tightly connected concepts. Difficulty in life feeds into hardship, and living in hardship makes things difficult. It's an unending cycle that can be broken, but rarely is. As we've already established, the early years of my life were dotted with a variety of difficulties, each of which helped to contribute to hardship in one form or another. This cycle sprang from one area of my life to another, and my relationships with the women in my life were no different. When the time came to "perform" as a man, I found it difficult, as my heart was carrying a heavy load from my days with my mother, aunts, and cousins. Part of the load in question was actually placed there by one of my cousins.

My mother and father both worked full-time jobs, so from time to time, this particular cousin would babysit me. Again, trust was placed in the sanctity of family bonds, and my safety was entrusted to her. Initially, whenever we were alone together in the family home, her care for me was innocuous enough. As time wore on, however, things began to change, largely through her actions whenever she came over. In those hours after school, before my parents would return, my cousin became the person who introduced me to sex. Actually, I think using the word "sex" suggests a level of innocence and consent, which was absent. I've tried to think of ways to phrase it more delicately, perhaps coating it in some euphemism or another, but I can't see what the use in that would be. Put simply, my cousin molested me.

The first time it happened, it seemed to come out of the blue. Nothing she had said or done in the time leading up to the event suggested that anything of the sort would ever come to pass. Regardless of notice, it happened. The two of us were in her bedroom one afternoon when she suddenly stood up and stripped off all her clothes before climbing under the covers of her bed. She then asked me to do the same. I obliged. She was older. She was family. Once I stood naked before her, she instructed me to join her in the bed, and lay down on top of her. Again, I obliged. She was older. She was family. Looking back on that day now, I suspect she could sense my confusion at the turn things had taken. In an effort to reassure me, she told me she loved me. She kept repeating this sentiment over and over again, explaining that this same love was the reason why we're doing what we we're doing. Not long after I was on top of her, she asked me to insert myself into her. Given my age, erections weren't yet possible, which she found frustrating. I recall crying at this point, though I can't be sure whether it was my inability to become aroused that brought on the tears, or the vague understanding I had that what was happening most certainly shouldn't be.

My tears fell well into the night after that first time, but they fell silently. Try as I might, I couldn't understand why she had become upset. I suspected that I was the cause and that I had done something wrong somehow, that I had *been* something wrong somehow. Despite the fact that so much wrongness was associated with what happened, I didn't tell my parents until much later in life. My hesitance came from many things, not the least of which was the fact that I associated love with sex for the longest time, something I still struggle with to this day. I was an incredibly loving child, wanting to care for everyone as much as I could. I would often run up to people and grab their legs, hugging them as tightly as I could. My mother would warn me against this, telling me that someone would someday take advantage of my loving nature, and I would be hurt. Naturally, I didn't believe her. But she was right. When the worst came to pass, and the advantage was taken, I was extremely confused. This confusion would last well into adulthood, as would all the misconceptions that came along with it.

# The Storyteller Within

Between the darker, heavier times of my childhood, I managed to carve out space for the discovery and cultivation of a passion. As part of the process of finding my footing as a person, I discovered the magic of storytelling. I can't recall the exact moment I was introduced to this medium or creative expression, but trust me when I say the experience had a powerful effect on me. You will remember my spellbinding, death-defying turn as Jezebel from the previous chapter. Along with this performance, there is another instance of storytelling as a child that sticks out in my memory. One year, in an elementary school production of *Pinocchio*, I was given the role of Jiminy Cricket. By this point, I already knew that telling stories and performing were things that made me excited, and that lay close to my heart. The role of Jiminy enthralled me in particular. Not only was I allowed to take to the stage once more—a real stage this time—but I would also be playing the physical embodiment of another person's conscience, a concept that thrilled me to no end. These early experiences with storytelling laid the foundation for a practice that would continue for years to come. As I grew older, I would continue to escape into other, fictional worlds in whatever way I could. I found that I was free to express myself within those pages or scenes. Later on, when things got bad in public school, I always had another place to go, another person to be, and another life to lead. Of course, this didn't solve my problems, but it made them just that extra bit more bearable.

Now, admittedly, this section is probably comparable to the briefest of footnotes found in academic journals. However, despite its brevity and lack of anecdotes further illuminating the state of my early years, sharing this information with you is of the utmost importance. Ambitious as it may sound, it is my hope that this section will have just as profound an impact on you as those that both precede and follow it. It may not make sense to tell you about my experiences embodying the characters of a biblical harlot or a small insect best known to the majority in its animated form, as depicted in countless children's films. However, there is sense to be found. Quite a lot of it, if you ask me. By sharing this part of myself, I wish to underscore the fact that the development of your true identity isn't contingent on rules, laws, or community values. The person you are will eventually make their way to the surface. Just because the people around you may not like who you are, or may even disallow the existence of someone like you in their presence, it doesn't mean that your identity will magically fade away. Instead, you will find yourself doing what I did: discovering new aspects of yourself and your life in secret. Each new discovery will be cloaked in normalcy, with its true impact known only to you. You will become who you are meant to be, regardless of where you are from or what is allowed. It can be exhausting to live in the shadows, this is true, but don't forget to explore the space around you a bit. You never know what may be hidden by the darkness, waiting to be brought to light to those who can see it.

# Fitting in With the Worldly People

As we leave my creative pursuits behind, we return once more to a concept that characterized so much of my life: masculinity. My introduction to the concept of gender came very early in life, with the various men in my family functioning as role models, demonstrating what a "true" man was meant to look, act, and sound like. From a young age, it was evident that I was never going to meet the criteria established by the religious conservatism I grew up with. However, the already tenuous grasp I held on masculinity became noticeably weaker as my time in the American school system wore on. More specifically, my perception of myself was greatly influenced by the caste system I encountered in middle school. Given where my school was situated in South Florida, boys my age were given two boxes in which to place ourselves. Once you had made your choice, you not only took on the style of that group's socialization, but you were also laden with all the perceptions, expectations, and biases associated with your part of the social system.

As a preteen, my choice of social association manifested in the form of a dichotomy. When my decision was made, I would either be a skater or a surfer. Now, admittedly, it may sound slightly absurd to place such a high level of importance on a label like this, but you have to understand how deeply these ideas were ingrained into our collective psyche. The division of people into predetermined categories was an important part of the community's functioning where I lived in South Florida. Not long after we arrived from New York, I was enrolled in school, and the question of my social allegiance was one of the first posed to me upon entering the school environment. Despite the urgency with which my decision was presented, I've never quite understood why it was necessary in the first place.

Naturally, I chose my clique—the skaters, for reasons we'll explore in a moment—but its existence as a prerequisite for my successful integration into the social scene is something that I've never been able to puzzle out. I understand its function as part of a larger desire for categorization, the type we find on a societal level. And yet, neither desire holds much water. Although I couldn't understand it, I still desperately did everything I could to find my place in the grand, social scheme of things. Though it may not have been clear to me at the time, this was my way of asserting my individuality. Doing this by becoming part of a pre-established collective might sound paradoxical, but bear with me for a moment. My attempts at becoming part of the masses were a declaration of individuality, at least as it pertained to the religious part of my life. As dictated by the teachings of the Jehovah's Witnesses, those who formed part of this religious body were meant to avoid associations with people who fell outside its bounds. Those who formed part of the latter category were known as "worldly people" and stood in direct contrast with those of us who were more spiritual due to our beliefs. The idea of this separation had been ingrained in my mind for as long as I could remember. And still, I was determined to do what I had to if it meant I could find my tribe among the more worldly kids. Call it determination or desperation; either way I tried my best to find those with whom I could not only survive, but also thrive. Navigating these treacherous social waters and choosing a clique was ultimately in service of fulfilling a desire I shared with just about everyone around me: wanting to belong.

As much as I would like to pretend that, because I made a choice and more or less understood the motivations behind my decision, the process of integration with my South Florida peers was seamless. Predictably, this wasn't the case. Even though I did an outstanding job of adopting the same beliefs regarding social hierarchy and the importance of categorizing my fellow preteens, something was still missing. This may come from the fact that the reasons why I had aligned myself with the skaters didn't resemble anything close to an interest in achieving the perfect 180 kickflip. To be fair, there was a measure of interest when it came to actually surfing the asphalt. However, this was informed by another part of my identity, one removed entirely from anything resembling ambitions in board-based athletics. I chose the skaters because they seemed to be the closest possible thing to what I already was, behaviorally speaking. In all honesty, the way they acted wasn't nearly close enough to how I did that I could just enter their ranks as myself and remain that way. I had to change to a certain extent, though that would have been true if I had chosen the oceanic board over its terrestrial counterpart. In addition to being somewhat connected to the person I was back then, skating held a very particular appeal: boys.

For my money, the skater guys were a lot easier on the eyes than the surfer dudes. So, to my still-developing mind, I was killing several birds with just one small, socially accepted stone. By becoming part of this group, I avoided becoming an outcast while simultaneously ensuring that my days were filled with eye candy. All things considered, I may also have found myself drawn to this group because I thought skating would be much easier to pick up than surfing. I had roller skated in the past, so I reasoned that these skills could be transferred to a board. More importantly, I figured this could be done easily. Needless to say, that impression didn't last very long. Actually, it only lasted until I saw all the tricks they could do, and was asked about what I was able to do with the board (spoiler alert: I could do just about nothing).

At some point, someone asked if I could "ollie," a question I answered with an entirely too confident "yes." Again, there was logic behind this response. I didn't have a skateboard of my own just yet, so I thought they would take my word for it. As you might expect, they didn't. The same person who asked about my abilities rolled over his board to me, asking me to show them what I could do. It will come as no shock that my subsequent attempt was a disaster and sent me straight back to the category of social misfit.

Of course, as toned and tanned as the aforementioned eye candy was, it was White in equal measure. This, too, made sense to me. The White skater boys I associated with were the pinnacle of manhood. They were everything I should strive to be, hoping that I would become more manly in the process—whether through osmosis or something else, I don't know. You have to remember that I had made it through a number of years by this point, and around every corner I had been informed that what I was should be rejected and corrected.

Within my household and religious community, this meant becoming less feminine. In society at large, this meant making myself appear to be as far from Puerto Rican (and queer) as possible. The way I reasoned it, by befriending the skaters, I was gaining access to a level of previously unattained, extremely aspirational Whiteness. Naturally, there was no way I could actually become the White boys I idolized so much. But by being close to them, and by being counted as one of them, I could get a hell of a lot closer to moving away from my place among the marginalized.

# The Middle Is the Most Awkwardly Troublesome

Now, not to make it sound as though my childhood was made up of only bad experiences, but I have to mention the fact that my acceptance went less than smoothly. No sooner had I assumed the moniker of skater when it was pointed out—quite accurately, in all fairness—that I was, in fact, not a skater. Of course, this revelation meant that I lost the little bit of social footing I had seemingly managed to find. However bad middle school had been up to this point, things became considerably worse. The bullying intensified—and once even escalated to physical violence—and my only refuge was my bedroom. There were a number of times when I came home from school and made a beeline for that door, shutting myself inside and crying until there were no tears left.

And yet, on the other side of the coin, this period of my life was marked with a number of significant changes, several of which tended toward the positive. Despite the fact that I was still tasked with navigating the fraught interpersonal dynamics of my family and the members of their religious community on a daily basis, it seemed that I was approaching some sort of equilibrium as I entered into adolescence. Though I had by no means figured out who I was (with or without the help of other adolescent South Florida skaters), my teen years surprisingly delivered an improvement in my relationship with my parents. Well, I'm not entirely sure we can call it an improvement. Let's say it was a *shift,* for want of a better term. The older I became, the more they began to trust me; the more they began to see me as someone they could entrust with more responsibility.

As the years crept on, my parents' perception of me changed. It started near the end of my time in middle school. I'm not sure what changed, but I was suddenly deemed adult enough to be able to handle having a glass of wine at dinnertime. Though something like this was simple enough, it meant a great deal to me. Alcohol was a distinctly adult substance, so the fact that I could consume it, however briefly, felt like I was unlocking a new level of life reserved only for those who could prove their maturity. Of course, being allowed this glass of wine wasn't the only thing that changed in these years. To my parents, it stood to reason that trusting me with alcohol meant that I could be trusted with other things, as well. For clarification, this meant that I could assume more responsibility for myself and my life, that I could understand why I ought to work more diligently, and that I could bear the consequences of misbehavior or ill-made decisions in the same way that any other adult could.

As wonderful as being seen through a lens of elevated maturity was, having my parents regard me as more of an adult meant that my mind began to move toward seeing myself in the same light. However, this posed a problem, as I was still light years removed from actual adulthood on just about every level—physically, mentally, and emotionally. Despite this, I found myself starting to move toward certain aspects of adulthood. More specifically, I demonstrated greater prowess at handling my identity, the way I thought adults had concrete, lasting control over theirs. Though I had in no way settled on the truth of who I was, nor found a space in which I could be myself without modification, restriction, or concern, I understood how to go about presenting myself to the world. By the time I entered my high school years, I had been disguising parts of myself for long enough to have developed something of a talent for hiding different aspects of myself to match whatever environment called for it. Through my time spent among the Jehovah's Witnesses, skaters, and people in general, I had learned to identify which mannerisms and characteristics were safe to express in a specific place, and which were best kept under wraps. Of course, there were certain parts of my identity I could never let slip, regardless of the company I kept. So, even though I held a tighter grip on who I was, it wasn't long before my hands grew tired and pained. But without anyone there to help, the pain became a fixture in my life. I never got used to it, but told myself I did, if only to spare my mind from lingering on the agony.

## Suppression Doesn't Solve Much of Anything

Continuing my rumination on the nature of my self-expression back in the day, I have to take a minute to acknowledge the fact that it was glaringly obvious that I was never going to fit in with those around me. However, as clear as this was, I still tried to push and fold myself into the mold I was given, the mold that was accepted and deemed desirable. This process was, of course, painful, and as little as I wished to undertake it, I understood it to be a necessary component in my survival. It was that same comprehension, that same necessity that saw me return to this effort time and time again, that saw me take who I was, crush it into a ball, and attempt to work it into the shape I was told it needed to be. I tried desperately to do away with the things that made me different. I tried to act more White to be accepted, to act more devout to be loved, and to be heterosexual to stay alive—and maybe even thrive. In the deepest parts of myself, I knew that I would never know romantic love for a woman, nor feel sexual attraction toward one. Still, I did everything in my power to lean into heteronormativity as much I could, fearing the smiting that I was terrified would be handed down should I act upon my feelings, or even have my thoughts linger on them too long.

Like so many other religious children, fear was what motivated me to strive for achieving the pinnacle of heterosexuality. I was afraid of what my parents and brother would think if they knew the truth of who I was. I was afraid of my extended family's rejection, of the hatred of my community, and of how my life would change if I ever had the courage to stand up, declare the truth, and remain something close to steadfast in who I was. More than anything else, the religious beliefs I held in my youth meant that I feared God, particularly the wrath I would face should I ever act on my most secret desires. Fear was a common thread linking many things in my life. Fear was also what kept me coming back to that mold time and time again. I was terrified at the prospect of losing what I had. Love was something I clung to and expressed as much as I could when I was a child. I loved anyone and everyone who would let me. If those same, loving individuals discovered the truth of my identity, I was all but sure that their hearts would turn to stone in a second. So I kept on trying to be something other than myself.

For all these efforts, for all these fears, and for all my determination that I would become what the world deemed acceptable, changing myself was anything but easy. Also, as I'm sure you've picked up on, those changes never really took. As much as I longed to be "normal," and to rid myself of worries regarding sexuality, attraction, and manliness, the parts of myself I hid from the world just wouldn't go away. To make matters worse, they soon became curiosities. I was confused about what these thoughts and feelings meant, due in large part to the fact that I never made an attempt to look at them for more than a few seconds.

That same fear we talked about a minute ago ensured that I ignored these feelings as best I could. Whenever I did interact with them, the experiences were shallow and fleeting. Consequently, my queerness became an alien abstraction—something I could imagine, and which I had a basic grasp of, but not something I could say I understood, at least not with any confidence. Everything I was suppressing became a question, and the desire for answers started to burn through my soul. I tried my best to avoid this, to adjust my heart so that it would be what I thought it should be. As one would expect, I never succeeded. There are many things we can do in life, and many things we have mastered through the millennia, but human beings are still woefully powerless against the forces of the heart. Within those chambers rested an incredibly strong yearning for the truth, for self-actualization, and for authenticity, even if it lasted only for a moment. When all is said and done, I'm still just human, and there was nothing I could do to push my heart in any other direction.

# Navigating High School Logistics

As I entered the white-water rapids of adolescence, there was nothing that could have prepared me for the near-constant barrage of changes that started on my first day of high school, ending only when I held my diploma safely in my exhausted hands. Being a teenager is, as most of us know, an absolutely awful experience tempered with moments of sheer glee, fleeting as they are. It's a time filled with uncertainty, ill-thought-out experimentation, and a desperate need (as well as some desperate attempts) to be anything but an outcast. It should be said that occasionally, when each of those things could be put to the side, some of the most fun experiences of my life took their place. It wasn't entirely bad. In fact, in those times when I could breathe, I also had the chance to do some of my best seize-the-moment living. In high school, there was nothing better than being a completely ordinary kid, just one of the masses. If you stood out in the wrong way, chances were you'd wandered from the beaten path in one way or another, and it was highly unlikely that you'd done so in a way that others would look kindly upon. Now, a lot of time has passed since I was a high school student—thank God, or whoever you think is out there—and I'm sure things have changed somewhat since the glory days of my youth. Nevertheless, that's what school was like in the '90s. As much as I'd like to paint a picture reminiscent of the very best music videos produced by the decade, the reality was different.

In high school, the dynamic between me and my parents continued to evolve. The closer I got to 18, the more they saw me as an adult. The tradition of a glass of wine at evening mealtimes that began toward the end of middle school continued and was one of the things that made me feel like I was legitimately inching my way toward being a proper adult. Of course, the closer I came to achieving this coveted state, the more panicked I became about the question of my identity. Despite my improved ability at hiding the real me, I still had very little idea who the real me actually was. As you can imagine, this led to a lot of feelings of confusion, feelings that simply compounded the unsure nature of adolescence that had already settled very neatly into my brain.

As luck would have it, I met someone during this time who would help me deal with so much of what I was struggling with—a great deal more than he was aware of. This person was a friend of mine, a classmate. We were the same age, had many of the same interests, and had even had similar experiences earlier in our lives. To top it all off, the person who would become the anchor and guiding light of my teenage self was, of all things, a Mormon. The irony is not lost on me, rest assured. His presence in my life reminds me of a passage from the

Bible that my father would use occasionally, and that I still quote to this day. The passage is 1 Corinthians 10:13: "No temptation has overtaken you except what is common to mankind. And God is faithful; he will not let you be tempted beyond what you can bear. But when you are tempted, he will also provide a way out so that you can endure it."

For the sake of privacy and efficacy, we'll refer to this friend of mine as "The Mormon." It's simple and potentially reductive, I'm aware, but I think concocting a bunch of aliases as I tell you this story would complicate matters unnecessarily. So, The Mormon and I became friends—best friends, actually. From the very first moment we met each other, something just clicked. Knowing what I know now, I think the reason for this strong, instantaneous connection lies in the fact that we were both struggling at the time. Though our lives were considerably different, both of us came from religious denominations that are considered to be somewhat odd by general society. Coming from that type of background can make it difficult to carve out a place for yourself in teenage society, especially when the element of hedonism enters partway through high school.

These types of activities were prohibited by each of our religious practices. However, because they form such a big part of the teenage experience, our abstention meant that there were experiences our peers were having that we just simply couldn't relate to, no matter how hard we tried. As disheartening as this sometimes was, we took solace in the fact that neither one of us were facing these feelings alone.

Let me be the first to say that, as beautifully as I do remember this friendship, I am well aware that telling a story beginning with a Jehovah's Witness and a Mormon sounds like the setup for an excruciatingly unfunny joke. With that out of the way, we can move on to the next "unconventional" aspect of my friendship with The Mormon: the fact that I fell in love with him; truly, deeply, and almost immediately. With the benefit and wisdom of time, I've come to learn that it's regarded as a sort of rite of passage, a young gay boy falling for his best friend. In these scenarios, the friend is almost exclusively heterosexual, thus enabling the manifestation of a coming-of-age experience, which subsequently allows queer boys everywhere to go forth and fall for straight men time after time. This was the paint-by-numbers nature of our friendship, as well. Predictably, the love I had for him could only ever exist in the form of hypotheticals in my mind and feelings of intense pining in my heart. The Church of Jesus Christ of the Latter Day Saints is many things, but queer-friendly does not rank among them (for the most part). Similarly, not much could be said for the Jehovah's Witness' embracing of same-sex love.

As debilitating as this conundrum initially seemed, I eventually moved past it. There was no way I could lose The Mormon as a friend. He was the most profound connection I held outside of my immediate family, and being with him (even just platonically) eased the burden of being a teenager, especially one who had previously always hovered on the precipice of isolation and loneliness. His presence played an essential part in establishing the happiness of my adolescence. Though things were far from perfect, my emotional state was in better shape than it had been in years. Along with his friendship, this shift was caused by the feeling I had that people were somehow more accepting in high school. In actual fact, I'm not sure if they actually were more accepting, or if people just focused less on others. The years between being a freshman and a senior were fraught with worry, longing, and difficulty. Looking back, I think my peers were too concerned with their own troubles and inner turmoils to notice that the shape of my masculinity and my heart didn't line up precisely with other boys my age. From a more optimistic point of view, this change may have occurred entirely within my mind. Maybe those around me did still care, but I didn't. Or, at least, I cared less than I had before, largely because I was steadily becoming more comfortable in my own skin. However, this feeling wasn't nearly strong enough for me to feel as though I could embrace the entirety of my identity. What I could embrace was reinforced by that perception of acceptance, which I won by making others laugh. Humor was my defense mechanism and my method of misdirection. If there was a way to make people see, hear, or otherwise perceive something funny, all the scrutiny they directed in my direction magically disappeared. If they were laughing, they couldn't look too closely, and if they couldn't look at me, they couldn't reject me. To my young mind, the absence of rejection was equal to the development of acceptance.

Still, despite this perception of acceptance (or, at the very least, apathy), there was still no way I could ask The Mormon to open his heart to me in that way. I may not have understood the exact nature of my attraction, but I understood that attempting to act on it could be disastrous. Regardless of this romantic setback, the years I spent in high school were markedly improved from their predecessors. This was due in part to that tighter grip I possessed, the one that held all the potentially upsetting or dangerous parts of myself firmly beneath the surface, away from anyone's eyes. Furthermore, I felt more confident in myself, to the point where it seemed to me that I commanded more of the rooms into which I entered and in which I existed. This is likely linked to my ability to better present the typical masculinity I had been pushed toward as a child. I had learned to alter my body language, to amend my posture, and to keep my legs apart, safely distancing myself from any effeminate poses that might cause consternation to anyone in my vicinity. I learned to observe myself and to correct any behavioral mistakes I made. My hands had previously given me away. Now, they were securely held by the side of my body, and their use was always carefully monitored by a part of my brain that would bring them down swiftly, should they ever become too animated.

By all appearances, my labors were working and were starting to pay off. People no longer sneered at me the way they had in the past. Increasingly, I was treated with less condemnation and was more readily embraced as all the other boys my age were. At least, this was the case in the secular spaces through which I regularly moved. In the more religious locales, acceptance still remained outside my grasp. Every time I went to the Kingdom Hall, the congregation's youth would do their absolute best to ensure that I understood myself to have been excluded from their group. The way they acted was reminiscent of my classmate's attitudes in middle school. They were determined to ostracize me from the rest of the kids my age, resolute to achieve their goal of keeping themselves as far away as possible from the "impurity" of my identity. There were exceptions, of course, but none that lasted very long. The few kids who didn't reject me outright, and who tried their best to embrace me were quickly brought into line by their parents, who kept them away from me and the bad influence these adults had convinced themselves I would bring into their children's lives. A lot of these parents' determination to steer their kids away from me came from the fact that anyone could see I had no real interest in the religion, nor in devoting my spare time in pursuit of spiritual development. At least not in the way they deemed appropriate. Of course, this was coupled with the fears they had developed that, should their children spend any amount of time with me, it was inevitable that I would change their kids in some terrible way.

Interestingly enough, everything they did seemed to contradict the teachings of the Jehovah's Witnesses. Though we had been taught that certain types of people were sinful and undesirable to liaise with, the institution had always maintained that its congregants should lead with kindness. According to what we had been taught, you could feel what you like about others, their actions, and their beliefs. However, condemnation or outright victimization was out of the question, as this made us no better than those who had strayed from the path of the Lord.

Nevertheless, these kids were determined to make me miserable. Actually, I can't say with complete confidence that this was their goal, or that my misery within the walls of the Kingdom Halls was caused by them alone. In truth, I think they were chasing the same type of acceptance I had pursued with the secular crowd. Within the confines of the religion, these kids were hell-bent on proving to their parents (and the congregation as a whole) that they were worthy of becoming the next, leading generation of Jehovah's Witnesses. This was their world, and these rules and conventions were all they knew. They were operating according to the truth they knew. In that way, I suppose we weren't so different.

Though their methods were largely the same, my fellow Witnesses differed from my middle-school harassers in a key way. The latter had sought to make me aware of my difference, and to ensure I knew there was no place for me among them. The children I met at the Kingdom Hall, however, sought nothing short of my destruction. They wanted to rip me apart spiritually, to cast out everything I was from the ground up. It was a sort of perverted bloodsport, one conducted under the auspices of piety and devotion to the word of God.

## One-and-a-Half Dozen and Out

Enduring these children's attacks on a regular basis leeched out quite a bit of the happiness I was starting to enjoy in adolescence. In an effort to make things better,

I tried to change and achieved some success. However, I never managed to make things as good as I would have liked them to be, though they were as good as they needed to be to get me to where I am today. This inability weighed on me, but I was fortunate enough to have someone who was willing to shoulder some of this emotional burden. Whenever I was experiencing difficulties, The Mormon was there, ready to comfort me and bring me into the safe embrace of our platonic bond. His effect on my mood (and on the way my heart would beat) was noticeable from the beginning. I tried to spend as much time with him as I could, if only to enjoy the comfort and peace I felt in his presence. Over time, as our bond grew, he allowed small acts of physical intimacy. From time to time, he'd let me rest my head on his shoulder, and after a while even allowed me to play with his hair on occasion. Though my heart was screaming for something more substantial than these small, innocuous points of contact, I found myself overjoyed at the prospect of receiving even that much from him.

This went on for a few years, with my love for him growing deeper and more painful with every day that passed. Eventually, it became impossible to keep the truth to myself, and I told him what I was holding in my heart all that time. In part, I did this to relieve the ache that had settled in my chest not long after our first meeting. However, I cannot deny that there was a (not insignificant) part of me that hoped my declaration would be met with an affirmation of his feelings, and my love would finally be requited. Despite my hopes, the universe interceded to remind me that things worth having are never easy to come by. The Mormon took what I said to heart, and never once made an attempt to dissuade me from my feelings, nor even to make me feel badly about the fact that I was attracted to men. In the same considerate way he had spoken to me throughout our friendship, he thanked me for my candor, told me he was flattered, and reminded me of his unwavering attraction to the opposite sex.

Truth be told, his response took me by surprise. Yes, I had hoped to hear that he felt the same way I did, but I had also considered only one other response outside of this. Although we had grown to be very close, and although I was young enough to think my fantasy could become reality, I was old enough to understand that that particular conversation could go very, very badly. Should he have failed to declare his undying devotion, I had fully prepared myself for the friendship to be lost. I expected him to become enraged, to scream at me, to demand I leave his life and never speak to him or look in his direction again. Of course, nothing The Mormon was could ever have resulted in this reaction.

Instead, he remained steadfast in his kindness, embracing me after I had divulged my feelings. Nothing could have prepared me for this, nor for what followed in the time after my revelation. The Mormon accepted who I was, without reservation and without condition. He was okay with who I was, The Mormon told me, and was happy I knew myself. Moreover, he informed me, he was just as sure of who he was, hence his inability to reciprocate my feelings. Though I must confess to being slightly disappointed that I hadn't managed to gain a boyfriend, I felt indescribable relief at the fact that I hadn't lost a friend.

The Mormon was the first person I ever told of the desires that I held at the very bottom of my heart. Though I was by no means ready to tell my family, his support and acceptance emboldened me to seek another way of being "out." I knew that I could never find what I sought there in the south of Florida, not as long as the world remained the way it was. However, there was I place I knew where people came together and lived as themselves, sheltered from the darkness of others by the glittering lights of their immense city. It was where I needed to go, if only to get a taste of authenticity. With this goal in mind, I finished my high school education, proudly wore my gap and gown, and soon after set off for the endless possibilities that would greet me when I arrived at the college in my original hometown: New York City.

Before we set off for the lights, glitz, and glamor of the Big Apple, there is one final story to tell of my South Florida days. More specifically, there is the story of my high school graduation to illustrate the nature of my journey at that point. I graduated in 1995, only a little while after the latest international smash-hit film from the House of Mouse hit theatres across the globe. This animated feature was none other than *The Lion King*, a film that would end up being my all-time favorite. With this lion-centered retelling of *Hamlet* taking the world by storm and dominating popular consciousness, it seemed only fitting that my high school principal decided that the topic for his graduation speech should be "hakuna matata." He used this Swahili phrase to send several hundred 17- and 18-year-olds out into the world, one that held a lot more worries than Simba and friends would have us believe. Nevertheless, the principal's words struck a chord with me. Though our stories were hardly the same, I couldn't help but see similarities between myself and the film's protagonist. When I threw my cap into the air on that summer afternoon, it marked the start of my journey. A few weeks later, when I left my family home in pursuit of my dreams, it was like I was making my own exit from the Pridelands to go and find a new territory, one that would hold the answers to all the questions I had about who I was—at least, I hoped it would.

# Chapter 3:

# An Identity for the Masses

So, with my first love having gently let me down, and with my secondary education finally completed, the world lay open before me. I was 18, excited, and hungry to get a taste of the world that lay beyond the confines of the Kingdom Hall and my family who frequented it. My eyes were full of stars, and my mind was full of ideas of what the future could be. This, along with all the clothes I could fit in my suitcase, were the only things I brought with me when I travelled north and began my new life as a college student in the Big Apple.

## Be It, Just Don't Act on It

Before we dive into my college years, it might be best for me to explain to you the motivation behind my choice of major. When I left Florida for New York, I went to pursue my dream of becoming an animator. Art had long been a passion of mine—a sort of combination of creative stimulation and desperately needed artistic expression. In fact, it was by far my favorite of all the classes I took in high school. For each of the four years I spent in the South Florida public–high school system, I made sure to have at least one art class. Of all the artistic styles and media I explored, nothing appealed to me more than animation, something that was helped in large part by my pure and undying love for the *Lion King*. My love for animation ran so deep that I was determined to be part of the sequel to Simba's saga I was convinced would eventually be made.

Although this medium wasn't exactly readily available to me in the public school system of the '90s, I discovered my love for it through drawing cartoons. Initially, I set out to replicate the style of Disney, setting my sights on becoming an animator for the famous House of Mouse and that glorious *Lion King* sequel. However, as my practice and exploration continued, I soon found myself deviating from that style in favor of creating my own. Such was my devotion to my craft that I was able to devise and copyright a cartoon of my own before I left high school. I was entirely sure that this was what I wanted my profession to be, so I applied to a school in New York, determined to pursue my artistic passions in a city that was teeming with culture. However, passion alone wasn't going to get me there, and I needed my parents to be on board with the idea before I could begin to imagine living my life in the city that never sleeps. To my astonishment, they were in favor of my career ambitions and gave me the go-ahead to move back north and start my adult life. I guess it's true that fortune favors the brave. Either that, or their permission was just the universe throwing me a bone, wanting me to be happy before discovering what lay in wait down the road.

Regardless of how it happened, it did, and no sooner had I graduated high school than my bags were packed and I was ready to begin carving out a place of my own in the world. As the start of the school year neared, I finally made my way to the city, moving in with my aunt and uncle. To prevent us from getting our wires crossed, I feel I should explain that this is a different aunt and uncle, not those who welcomed my family to South Florida all those years before. They were very welcoming of me, and I must confess that there was something comforting in having family members nearby as I ventured out into the world as an adult for the first time. However, as wonderful as it was staying with them, I was dead set on making the most of my newfound freedom and doing all the things I never dared to while living under the watchful gaze of my parents, extended family, and the entire Jehovah's Witness community of southern Florida.

One of the ways in which I first asserted my freedom was by picking up the habit of smoking cigarettes. To be perfectly honest with you, to this day I'm still unsure why I decided to start smoking. I never had any desire to do so before, nor had the need for nicotine overtaken me when I moved to New York. I suppose I should chalk it up first and foremost to how desperately I wanted to show everyone around me that I was no longer a child. Apart from this, my smoking may very well have been motivated by contextual and environmental factors. After all, I was an art student in a city known for its chic bohemian denizens. Even as a newly minted adult, I still desperately wanted to fit in. If that meant leaning into some of the cliches surrounding artists and their vices, so be it, as long as they would claim me as one of their own.

In addition to demonstrating my independence by means of cigarettes, I also sought to live a life that held more of the experiences that would affirm my identity. This was facilitated through the use of what can be described as the first versions of social media, if I'm being generous. Though the technology was still miles away from what we have today, it did the job. In this case, the job was connecting me with other gay men around the city. I would seek their company as often as I could, reveling in the fact that I was finally able to be with people like me, who wanted to do the same things I did. Once or twice, the circumstances under which I met these men were less than ideal, but then again, there wasn't very much we could expect when it came to security during secret hookups. Regardless, I felt more alive in those first few months back in New York than I had felt in years living down south. And yet, there was still something not quite right with my bliss, something that wasn't all that difficult to pin down.

Despite the fact that I was living as close to my authentic self as I ever had, everything I did, I did in secret. My family didn't know I smoked, and they absolutely didn't know that I was exploring the activities of the queer community. As happy as it made me to finally be able to do all these things, doing them behind closed doors and in places where nobody I knew would discover them weighed heavily on me. I had been excited for the fresh start that college offered, and yet there was very little I could actually do to live as I had dreamed of living. There were times when it felt as though I had imagined all the progress I'd made. There I was, out of my parents' house, chasing my dreams, and keeping the same secrets I'd had when I was younger. For all the excitement and exploration, I couldn't help but focus on the lack of openness in my life. Of course, as time wore on, this too became something I tried to incorporate into my new, exciting existence. It stood to reason that, if I couldn't do what I wanted out in the light of day, I should take advantage of all the night had to offer.

# The Artist Within

My freshman year of college was all about living like the artists I had read about and seen in the movies. This meant trying as many new things as I could. While we'll get to the new activities in a minute, it's worth pausing to look at something I had carried over from my high school days. Back in Florida, I had regularly snuck out of my parents' house to meet men, many of whom were considerably older than I was. At the time, this didn't faze me, as what we did together was the only thing that kept me tethered to the part of myself I had become so good at hiding from the world. These illicit rendezvous were the first time I had come into contact with the world of sexual activity after those encounters with my cousin when I was younger. With the benefit of hindsight, I understand now how harmful each of these meetings were. Every time I went to see a new man, my understanding of what sex was became more and more clouded. Eventually, this spilled over into what I thought love was. Though it didn't happen with each one, I found myself falling for several of the men I saw under these mysterious circumstances. However, because our relationships—if you could call them that—were centered around sex, I soon began to conflate this concept with that of romantic love, and I still held onto this muddled comprehension when I left for college. There, in New York, I would only become more confused. Sex was readily available to me, yet love remained out of my reach. Still, I was determined to find it despite the fact that I wasn't all that sure what love really was. I understood New York to be the place where everything could be found if you went to look for it, and look I did.

If you'll recall, I was determined to lean in to the carefree, bohemian life I felt an artist like me ought to live. It was this intention that led me to the world of substances, one in which I would come to establish near-permanent residence over the course of several years. My first steps on this downhill path were bolstered by the first type of alcohol I had ever consumed. In the taste of wine, I found a comforting familiarity accompanied by the burning sensation of numbing escapism the liquid had provided me since that first glass at my parents' dining room table. But as comforting as this feeling was, it served only to tie me to the past, so I decided to use it instead as a point of entry. I was familiar with wine and had been for a while. Because I could still remain relatively stable after a few glasses, it stood to reason that I could start working my way into the world of heavier, more intoxicating drinks.

This is how I came to find liquor—true, hard liquor— the type that burns through your body as if attempting to incinerate every part of you that was too unpleasant, unclean, or immature. Of course, this internal fire was accompanied by a number of other effects, all of which I enjoyed immensely. One such effect was the sudden stimulation of courage and impulsivity. Drinking made me feel good, made me feel like the adult I knew I was. So, I reasoned, if I could unlock that part of my identity with these spirits, why not wield them to explore other things, as well? Thus, liquor became my companion on my nighttime excursions into the world of the gay man's New York, and what an excellent wingman the substance proved to be. The more I explored, the more I learned, and the more pleasure I experienced. It felt like I was, at long last, living life the way it ought to be lived.

After so many years of fear, repression, and secrecy, letting loose (although still not entirely) was, at the time, the best thing that ever happened to me. I had never known happiness like this, and I never wanted to part from that feeling. Separating from that sensation meant going back to my real life and toiling away at my future again. Since I had no desire to feel anything but good, I began to lose interest in my schoolwork, the very thing I had been so excited to start working on mere months ago. My rapid loss of investment was helped in large part by the illegal license I had managed to obtain a while before, and which allowed me to gain entry to all the bars and clubs with which I had become so preoccupied, and which were keeping me away from my education.

Describing the shift in my attitude as simple disinterest would be something of a misrepresentation. It wasn't that I wanted to abandon my studies entirely, or that I had lost any of the passion I held for my dreams.

Rather, I felt awkward every time I went to class. More specifically, I felt awkward every time I went to acting class. Now, if you're confused about why someone who was majoring in visual art with the aim of becoming an animator would take an acting class, you're in the same boat I was back then. I couldn't understand why it was necessary for me to study acting. My confusion was further compounded by my attendance of classes in which I not only learned about the history of motion pictures but also had to read passages from the Bible (possibly to connect the two, but who knows?). This latter avenue of study was especially frustrating considering how hard I had worked to move beyond the borders of the Kingdom Halls and their larger institution. Because I could in no way make sense of what these things had to do with one another, I began to feel as though it was almost like God himself was laughing at me and my attempts to escape.

Regardless of whether I was actually the target of divine mirth, I was unhappy. I wanted to draw cartoon characters—nothing more, nothing less. In due course, I would learn that acting was an essential component of learning how to be an animator. Drawing those characters, whatever they were doing or whatever they looked like, meant drawing human behavior. In turn, this meant understanding human behavior, something that was linked not only to animation projects, but to the entire industry in which I hoped to make a name for myself. Of course, I didn't know this at the time, so I remained upset. I was 18 and I thought, *I'm in a new city with new people, exploring new things and becoming the person I was meant to be*. I didn't want to bother with useless classes like this, especially not if the time spent there took me away from the exciting world into which I had only just set foot. Now, not to make excuses for myself, but I was 18 when my mind followed—and religiously stuck to—this train of thought. I was quite literally still a teenager. As such, I decided not to yield to the will of those who sought to waste my time. I wanted to be out in the world, falling deeper and deeper in love with the community I'd found. But my education was keeping me away from this. So, in retaliation, I decided I would go to acting class, after all. I went to the others, too, albeit begrudgingly. But even though I attended, I vowed that I would not like it at all. They could force my attendance, but they could not force my interest. I'm slightly embarrassed to tell you that I felt quite smug about this plan, thinking I had done something so fantastically antiestablishment. There are truly very few things in this life that can match the stupidity of a teenager.

I'm sure it'll shock you to learn that my ingenious form of rebellion never really amounted to much. The closest I ever came to actually subverting anything was on the first day of acting class. As a sort of introductory icebreaker, the teacher went around the class, asking each student who their favorite actor or actress was. After naming them, the person then had to justify their answer. Steadily, the teacher made her way through the group, asking and listening as each person named their favorite performer. Everyone who went before me gave incredibly impressive answers, listing off phenomenally talented A-listers. Finally, my turn came. The teacher posed the question once more, and without really thinking too much about it, I told her my favorite actor was none other than Kermit the Frog. Predictably, my answer was met with silence and the shocked stares of my classmates. I was aware that the attention fixed on me wasn't necessarily a good thing, but I still liked being the one on whom everyone's gaze was fixed. Of course, my teacher had to ask the follow-up. I explained that I liked Kermit because he wasn't a person, and I wasn't all that fond of actors. Though not entirely intentional, I lost any and all chance of impressing my teacher the moment I uttered those words. She didn't particularly care for my answer, and I don't think I was ever able to redeem myself in her eyes. Although I can't be sure, I have a suspicion that she just saw an amphibious green puppet every time she looked at me. Even if acting class is a place where anything goes, that's not really ideal, is it?

## An Actor Prepares

In this time, my life became a whirlwind of classes, drinking, partying, and sex—there was very little of substance happening in my life. I was barely holding on when it came to studying, and the more hedonistic part of my life grew increasingly frenzied. I presumed that this was normal for a student. I'd heard how much of a party college could be, and I wanted to partake in that as much as I could. So, with control over my life pretty much nowhere in sight, I let things go on, just doing my best to make it through each new day that dawned.

Then, one day, I found myself in the school library. Now, if reading that shocks you because of what we've learned regarding my penchant for doing anything other than studying, you will be forgiven. However, I will have you know that I was quite the scholar as a child—or, at the very least, a well-read, scholarly student. Apart from my desire to make my parents proud, my voracious consumption and analysis of literary works emerged as a byproduct of what was then my religious practice. As a Jehovah's Witness, reading the Bible and other religious literature was incorporated into my schedule from a young age. As adherents of the faith, we were meant to study and interpret holy texts as well as supplemental materials several times a week. As it transpired, this particular dogmatic ritual ensured that I developed a deep love for reading and literature. From a young age, I knew the power the written word held, and was in awe of its potency and potential. As a result, on that particular day, I suddenly found myself drawn to the place where words and their power were kept.

To this day, I feel there's something magical about places like libraries, where you're surrounded with so many books containing so much powerful knowledge. Back in the day, however, it was odd that I went there, as it wasn't something I'd made a habit of. I usually made a beeline for the door once my classes were finished, eager to start my nightly process of inebriation. That day, however, I wandered into the stacks, and I thank God (or whatever forces or beings that may have been listening) that I was sober enough to pick up a book. The book in question wasn't a tome by any means, but it might as well have been for all the impact it would come to have on me. By happenstance, I had spotted a book on acting and felt compelled to see what was inside. As it transpired, the book was the first of a trilogy known as the *ABCs of Acting*. Written by Konstantin Stanislavski, the book was titled *An Actor Prepares*, and it outlined the internal, exploratory process actors must undertake when preparing for a role, as devised by the author's famous system. To this day, I remain mystified by the fact that I was drawn to that particular book, but I nevertheless cracked the cover, began reading, and felt myself enveloped by a feeling of sudden, overwhelming profundity. I'm not sure what that was, either, but I believe it's the closest I will ever come to actual divine intervention.

Every word Stanislavski had written resonated with me deeply. With every paragraph that passed, I felt myself becoming more and more enamored with the art of acting. I couldn't put the book down, couldn't let it go, so I checked it out and dove straight back in the moment I got home. The more I read, the more incredulous I became at the beauty of this craft, and the more regretful I became at the thought of having dismissed it for so long. No sooner had I turned the last page than I rushed back to the library to check out every book I could lay my hands on about this topic. As I tore through volume after volume, my excitement only grew, and I eventually found that I couldn't keep it to myself. The first time I returned to class after my discovery, I shared my enthusiasm with everyone who was within earshot. I proclaimed that class to be the greatest I had ever taken, and could not stop gushing about my love for the subject. In retrospect, my classmates may have suspected some sort of psychotic break, though they never expressed anything more than incredulity at the fact that I had had such a quick and comprehensive change of heart. Despite their doubts, my love for acting showed no signs of dissipating anytime soon. In fact, it had taken hold of me so tightly that I genuinely considered changing my major. I never did, but came close enough for me to be sure that I did, indeed, love the art of acting.

As wonderful as this turn of events was, it's worth remembering that this was real life, after all, and things couldn't stay too stable or too healthy for too long, at least not back then. In that time, my appreciation for acting wasn't the only thing that saw a sharp increase. Although I had tried on several occasions to cut my social activities down to something that could generously be deemed manageable, despite my efforts, I found myself venturing into the world of strobing lights, writhing bodies, and illicit substances time and time again. Each time, my return would be different, and my desire to leave those wondrous, intoxicating places became less and less. In the end, it became apparent that this was one battle I wasn't going to win.

So, as a solution, I decided to move out of my aunt and uncle's house, and into the apartment of my paternal uncle. All this time, I had been commuting back and forth from Staten Island. Now, however, I would be taking up residence in Manhattan, right in the thick of all the New York action. By moving, I reasoned, I was cutting down on travel expenses, and my closer proximity to school would also ensure a boost in my academic performance. This was the reason I gave my family, and it was true...in part. On the other side of the coin, however, was the fact that living in Manhattan would bring me that much closer to the places and people who populated the city's nightlife, something which I myself had become a denizen of as well. I'm sure there's a pithy remark to be made here about beating them and joining them, but I'll leave that to you.

As an aside, and to demonstrate just how deeply the love of acting settled into my bones, it's worth telling you that my undergraduate major was, in fact, acting for the theater. There are many stories to be drawn from this time, and almost all of them remind me of the severity of my drinking, and consequently make me wonder how on Earth I made it all the way through to graduation. One such example can be found in my experience playing God in a play called *Corpus Christie*, which presents an alternate Biblical reality in which each of the 12 apostles who followed Christ were gay. Being put on at a public university, our production drew a lot of attention, particularly from the state department, who made an attempt to shut us down once they got wind of it.

Despite their efforts, we would not be deterred. The matter garnered quite a lot of media coverage, resulting in us having to wade through crowds of reporters just to make our call times, or to get to the theater in time to warm up for our rehearsal. To this day, it's one of the most high-profile events I've been a part of, and it's had a lasting impact on me. Regrettably, I remember very little of this experience outside of the media circus. The most I can recall is stumbling through a few performances. Everything else has been lost to time.

# Everything and the Kitchen Sink

My move to Manhattan took place about halfway through the second semester of my freshman year. Hard as it may be to believe, all these ups and downs had come to pass in only about six months. The first year of college wasn't even over yet, and my life had become unrecognizable when compared with the existence I led under the watchful eye of my parents just months prior. Among the myriad of things that had changed was my physique. Not long after my discovery of Stanislavski's work, I landed a job at a Manhattan gym. As a perk, I could use the gym's facilities, something I decided to take full advantage of. Given my dedication to my craft, I was determined to make myself look just like all those A-listers my classmates had named at the beginning of the year. To my mind, looking like a famous actor meant that I was one step closer to claiming the title legitimately. Achieving this goal meant that I threw myself into exercise with perhaps slightly too much gusto. It wasn't long after I had begun my stint at the gym when trouble arose. In breaking with previous patterns, I wasn't ostracized by my coworkers or deemed to be different in some way from any of the people working out around me. This time, the obstacle wasn't external in nature, and the seed of trouble began blooming in my heart. To be more precise, it began in my chest, with pains that didn't debilitate me, but that were still sharp enough to be immediately noticeable.

At the risk of making excuses for my past self, I do feel it bears repeating that I was still a teenager at the time.

From the idealistic, I'm-too-young-to-have-issues-like-these perspective I occupied, these pains were refused the chance to take up any real estate in my consciousness. Instead, I chalked their manifestation up to my sudden adoption of an intense workout regimen and reasoned that they would go away with time, probably as my body became more used to these activities. Despite my youth, I was old enough to understand that having pains like these wasn't normal. However, the pros outweighed the cons in this instance; at least, they did in my mind. If we follow my logic, working out was the key to everything. The fitter I became, the more men I could attract, and the more I could experience what I believed to be authentic love.

Moreover, the better my physical shape, the more seriously I would be taken as an actor, the further I could explore the craft, and the sooner I would become a legitimate artist. If you haven't guessed yet, my inexpert opinion about medical issues did, in fact, prove to be incorrect. Believe me, I was just as shocked as you are now. Regardless of my initial error in judgment, the pain persisted. Weeks and eventually months passed, and the pangs in my chest never faded, no matter how accustomed the rest of my body became to the hours I spent in the gym. As time wore on, the pain became worse, and my confusion deepened. Still, I didn't seek help. Eventually, it grew to the point where the simple act of breathing became difficult, with sharp pains slicing through my chest every time I inhaled. I started suffering from terrible insomnia once the pain became this bad. I'd lie in bed at night, unable to fall asleep, unable even to move as the agony of breathing refused to go away.

# When the World Stops

After a few months of sleepless nights, painful days, and an increasingly urgent, gnawing feeling, I decided to pay my doctor a visit. After the initial exam, I was subjected to a number of different tests, and an X-ray scan before being told to come back for the delivery of my results. For better or worse, I decided to appeal to my doctor before I left the consultation room. I told him of the immense pain, emphasizing the fact that it had grown so intense that there were times when I could no longer move the way I was meant to. After stating my case, I was handed a prescription for painkillers. A temporary fix, I was told, one that would provide me with muscle relaxers and other numbing agents for a full two weeks.

After that, the doctor informed me, my results would be ready, and we would plan the way forward from there. With the promise of finding some answers on the horizon, off I went with my prescriptions, hopeful that the medication would do its job. As it happened, the painkillers did nothing more than dull the sensations that ran like daggers through my chest. At a loss, in agony, and unable to secure stronger dosages, I turned to the only other thing I knew would help to deaden my nerve endings so I couldn't feel what was happening in my chest. I had continued partying and drinking all this time, and had become well-accustomed to the world of alcohol. I knew the effect it had on me, and hoped that that same effect would now manifest, this time in conjunction with those already being produced by the pills.

For the remainder of the two weeks, I was out of my mind. I stuck to the doctor's prescription, dutifully swallowing pills as directed. Additionally, I was administering my own home remedy with the same consistency. The painkillers, muscle relaxers, and spirits all mixed inside my body, ensuring that I could not feel the pain—or much of anything else, truth be told. I was so dead to the world that the call from my doctor, summoning me back to his practice, inspired nothing more than an apathetic reply and an agreement to make an appointment. I had no idea how much time had elapsed when he called, and when the day came that I had to go see him, I have no recollection of how I ended up sitting in his office, never mind making it through the city to see him. And yet, one emotion did manage to break through the haze of substances that were clouding my mind. I was angry with my doctor, something I expressed to him by slamming the bottle of pills down on his table when he entered.

As I say this, I realize that there must have been some measure of premeditation on my part, given that I had the presence of mind to take the bottle with me when I left my uncle's apartment. Perhaps the pills and booze didn't make me as numb as I thought they did. Maybe there was a part of my brain, the part that remained more or less sober, that knew something wasn't right, and that hid my consciousness from the world. However it came to pass, it did, and I informed the doctor of my fury. I relayed their inefficacy, telling him that they did nothing else but make me feel drunk and high. In light of what he knew, it made sense that my doctor all but dismissed my complaints. He understood, naturally, that my state wasn't brought on by painkillers alone. But perhaps he knew that this was the lesser of two evils that had to be dealt with. The bigger evil was one I would encounter very soon. Our second meeting would occur only minutes after my dramatic entrance, when my doctor's face fell into an expression of grave stoicism, and his voice directed me to sit down, as there was a different, much more important matter to discuss.

# Chapter 4:

# A Mass Conspiracy

On the tail end of a bender, I was called into the doctor's office, and I received news that would change my life forever. As I look back on that day now, decades later, I still have so any questions. Why was this the news I received? Why was this happening to me? Why was I the one who had been saddled with this burden? Of course, these questions arise alongside ideas that I could have done something different, something better. However, as each query rolls by, I'm reminded of the fact that the past is the past. I could no more change what happened in that office than I could alter the makeup of my genes, or control the way in which the cosmos continues to spin.

## Mass Conspiracy

Even though so many years have passed, I can still recall the scene that day in my doctor's office with striking clarity. I sat in silence after his announcement of a more serious matter. It seemed as though I sat for centuries and as if no time passed at all before he mounted my X-rays onto the light box fixed on the wall. Once the scans were clipped into the contraption, things started to pick up speed, and the ball was soon rolling faster than I was able to keep up with. With the precision afforded to him by his years as a clinician, my doctor pointed to the part of the X-ray where the middle of my chest lay, where the image had become fuzzy, almost distorted. There, he informed me, smeared across the scan in a white haze, was a mass. In the same breath as he delivered this news, he also informed me that things had progressed to the point where I needed to have surgery immediately. Apparently, the situation had become so emergent that he needed to put me on his books as soon as possible, potentially wheeling me into the operating room the very next day.

To his credit, the doctor hadn't seemed as though he wanted to overwhelm me, but his probable intention, unfortunately, didn't match his words. I desperately wanted time to stop, for the world to be put on pause so I could have a moment to deal with what I'd been told—or to try, at the very least. But nothing stopped, nothing even wavered. The world kept on turning, my heart kept on beating a mile a minute, and my doctor kept on making arrangements for the procedure. The more he talked about availability and scheduling surgeries, the more my head felt as though it was going to explode, more than likely taking my heart along with it. Though it couldn't have been more than a minute, I felt like I was enduring a years-long sonic assault, and I couldn't take any more of it.

I don't exactly remember what I said or did, but I recall bursting out of my doctor's office and running as though my life depended on it. I had no idea where I was going, but I needed to get out of that building, to feel the air of the city on my face. I made it out onto the street and began walking down the sidewalk. I had no destination, only determination. However, for all the distance I hoped to put between me and that godforsaken place, I had no idea where I was going. By this point, something had started to kick in, and tears poured from my eyes faster than they could fall. Soon, my vision became so clouded that I couldn't see anything around me—not the cars that rolled by, the pedestrians I bumped into, or even the sidewalk I was stepping on so hurriedly.

As you can imagine, my mind refused to stand still, and I was soon spiraling deeper and deeper, finding my thoughts drifting further and further from anything logically pertaining to the world of medicine. This was coupled with confusion and several layers of heavy, profound doubt. All of this condensed into a multitude of questions, the worst questions I had ever asked in my life. What was happening inside my body? Why wasn't I able to control what was going on? What was growing inside myself? Where would I go from here? What would my life become? From out of the mist cast over my brain by all these panicked questions, one rose above all the others: Was I being punished for who I was? After all my years as a God-fearing Jehovah's Witness, I had stepped into the secular world with much gusto and had reveled in my time away from the church, its doctrines, and the word of the Bible. Though I hadn't spent very much time removed from traditional religious teachings—less than a year—was this how I was being roped back into the flock? Had God, in all his infinite wisdom and justness, actually done something to me or otherwise allowed something to happen to me, all because I didn't feel the type of love that his other children did? All these thoughts were marching through my mind in quick succession, leaving no room for resolution or even proper acknowledgement. And yet, the deeper I fell into this rabbit hole of existential doubt and self-blame, the more sure I became that I had, in fact, grabbed the right end of the stick. I knew that who I was and the things I wanted were wrong, and had been told as much on multiple occasions throughout my childhood. Still, I had made it to adulthood by refusing to make the changes I was told were needed. I tried, but I couldn't help myself. I just couldn't steer my heart, mind, or body in the direction society and religion had directed me. More than anything else, I was sure that this was the punishment I was receiving for my willful deviation from the norm.

My head continued to reel, and my heart grew heavier with the certainty that I had brought this on myself. Ironically, all this certainty meant that I was also plunged deep into feelings of uncertainty. I had no idea what lay ahead, nor what I was meant to do after getting this news. Though the mass in my chest hadn't yet been labeled as cancerous, I had an inkling of what was growing inside me, and I understood that no part of my life would be exempt from this illness. I knew that whatever came with whatever was inside me would affect not only my mind, body, and soul, but would also touch the lives of my family, as well as hamper my ability to work and pursue the dreams I had held in my heart for such a long time. These were the things I knew, but they seemed small in comparison to all the things I had no idea about. And this feeling was enough to erase all of the adulthood I had managed to hold on to. My first instinct was to call my parents, possibly to see if there was anything they could do to make this all go away. While they couldn't offer me a miraculous recovery, they could put me on the next plane back home. So I raced to the airport, climbed aboard that flight that would take me to South Florida, and sent myself careening back into the familiar, stable, and comforting embrace of my family.

# His Name Was Hodgkin's Lymphoma, Sent From God

My return to South Florida, while not the permanent solution part of me had hoped it would be, proved to be just what I needed to jolt me back to reality. Naturally, my parents were worried sick when I showed up on their doorstep with a chest full of something that was yet to be categorized and nearly out of my mind. Of course, as hard as the news hit them, both my mother and father remained parents, and ones who had just about mastered their craft at that. All of us were terrified, but they never allowed themselves to sink into the same pit of panicked despair I had fallen into so soon after receiving the news—at least, not in front of me. Interestingly, their resilience and comfort was something I found to be present in other members of my family and the community, as well. Moreover, what I didn't find in these same people was something I had expected to be greeted with the minute they discovered the state of my health. Not one of the people with whom I shared my diagnosis turned to the assignation of blame as a means of explaining or justifying my condition. Where my mind had thought only of pointing all the fingers toward myself, others all informed me that cancer was something that happened. It was an illness that developed in some, but not in others; there's nothing much to be done about it—at least not before you know it's there. Hesitant as I was to accept what I thought was simple placation, I ultimately decided to accept the fact that this was simply a chapter in my life's story that had to be read, and there were no two ways about it. I should admit, in the interest of transparency, that my acceptance wasn't complete. There was still a considerable part of me that remained convinced that this was some form of divine retribution. My most compelling piece of evidence? The fact that I had just begun to live my life the way I had always wanted to, that I had just given into the thing I had avoided and ignored for so long (the gay thing, in case you got lost) when this particular diagnostic boulder was rolled across my path.

Speaking of diagnoses, I suppose this would be a good time to tell you how I finally learned the formal, proper label for what was happening inside my body. Upon my return to my hometown, I shared the news with my family, who of course became very concerned about my condition. It was this concern that motivated me to seek medical attention once more. All I knew was that I had a mass growing inside me, and while I knew enough to understand that things like this were usually cancer-related, a formal diagnosis and prognosis were still required. My new doctor performed a biopsy and delivered two pieces of news when he laid out the results for us. The first of the two was that the mass that had been identified in my chest was indeed a tumor. However, where my doctor back in New York had correctly made this identification, what he hadn't told me was that the mass was in fact two separate tumors, one being significantly larger than the other. The second bit of news delivered was that the masses had been examined, and they were indeed cancerous. More specifically, the classification provided by the lab results was that of Hodgkin's lymphoma. To close out what was possibly the bleakest debriefing of my life, my doctor informed us that my cancer had progressed, and my formal diagnosis was that of stage IV Hodgkin's lymphoma. It's important to understand that this was stage four of four. There was nowhere for the severity of my condition to go. This was final boss-level cancer, when your only options are to beat the villain or accept the fact that the game is over. Listen, this diagnosis was hard to receive, but on the bright side, you can't accuse me of ever doing anything half-heartedly. If I was into something, I was into it with all I had. I knew this about myself, but didn't expect this particular aspect of my personality to spill over into quite so many parts of my life.

It may come as a surprise to you to learn that, against the backdrop of all these grim tidings, something that stood out to me more than I thought it would was how my doctors acted when speaking about my cancer. The first thing that baffled me was the fact that every description of my tumors was delivered in the form of a sports analogy. Perhaps the most memorable were the metaphors used during the appointment when I received my diagnosis. My doctor informed me that the larger of the two tumors was roughly the same size as a standard football. The smaller tumor, he continued, was round and about the same size as a golf ball. The irony of this imagery wasn't lost on me, given the fact that sports and I had never seemed to be on the same page. In addition to being confused by the connection made between sports and my diagnosis, I was also surprised by how casually each clinician I spoke to talked about my cancer, as well as the ways in which it would be treated. When I first heard the prognosis, I was struck by the matter-of-factness with which it was conveyed. In hindsight, they may have been trying to ease my mind, especially given how young I was. However, their statements telling me how often they did this type of work, and how regularly they encountered this illness did little to alleviate my concern, and in my already emotionally wrung-out state, made them seem dismissive of what I was going through. Moreover, I was told by the doctors that all I would have to do is make it through six months of chemotherapy. Was it intense? Yes. But I just had to make it through, and everything would be okay. As good as I'm sure their intentions were, their words did little to relieve the pressure that was weighing so heavily on my heart.

I think part of the problem I had with the way my doctors talked about the cancer stemmed from the fact that I never quite let go of the idea that my diagnosis was some form of punishment handed down from above. Consequently, when each of my doctors (the people who held the course of the rest of my life in their hands) were so flippant about the cancer and its progression, my issues with God added their voices to the ever-increasing chorus filling my head. To me, it seemed as though they were the manifestations of the aforementioned deity—or, at the very least, people who regarded themselves as wielding the same level of power—and they were entirely convinced that they were able to control something as malicious, unpredictable, and stubbornly alive as cancer. It felt very much like the doctors were so self-assured when it came to their knowledge and skills that they entirely failed to take into account that I didn't know the things they did, nor could I do the things they could. To me, it looked very much like they were these gods floating above the state of my body and soul, ready to implement whichever plans they saw fit, doing so with the severity they thought best. Of course, I wasn't consulted in this, only instructed.

# Learning What "Aggressive" Means

The gods had spoken, and the resolution had been handed down from the heights of their expertise: I was to undergo six months of intense, regular chemotherapy as the primary means of combatting the cancer flowering inside my chest. This decree terrified me, in large part due to the fact that I had no idea what chemotherapy actually was or how it worked. I understood that there was something going into my body, and had surmised from the first part of the word that what was going in would be chemical in nature. Apart from that, I had no idea what to expect. That's not to say that I didn't know anything about chemotherapy at all. Despite the fact that I hadn't ever thought much about it, I had heard time and time again that the process had the potential to become deadly. Pumping large quantities of chemicals into the human body is expected to produce the potential for some pretty severe side effects, I suppose. Going into the process knowing this, I was terrified. Unfortunately, this was just about the only thing I could say I knew about chemo, its substances, how it worked, and what the outcome would be. In fact, I knew little about cancer as a whole. I'd never thought to delve into the subject, and so every new piece of information was met with feelings of worry, fear, and hesitance. I think my apprehension wasn't helped much by the fact that my doctors kept telling me that things were as simple as making it through the treatment. They told me I shouldn't worry, and that my focus should lie only in dealing with the chemo sessions and getting through those six months. Unsurprisingly, I was still worried. Aside from what I knew about chemotherapy, I was also walking from day to day carrying the weight of those two tumors inside my chest. On top of that rested the heaviness that came with trying to live through the final stage of cancer.

Spending every day bogged down by all of this became much too heavy a burden to bear, and I started searching for a way to make things better. Naturally, I knew that I couldn't improve my situation in any significant way, but I could at least find something that would ease a bit of that weight off my heart. Finally, I decided that the way to deal with my diagnosis was to find out more about it. I'd never paid much attention to things like cancer or chemo, so it stood to reason that my lack of knowledge would result in my feeling overwhelmed. Unfortunately, my plan didn't go nearly as smoothly as I'd hoped. All around me were people willing to provide information, tips, and resources, which in and of itself wasn't a bad thing at all. The trouble came in with the number of people who stood at the ready. What they had to offer was much more than I expected, and I had no idea how to find a point of entry so I could start working my way through the mountain of information there seemed to be on the subject of lymphoma and its associated treatments. At one point or another, I think my brain broke a bit; I decided to take in what I could, and handle the rest on a case-by-case basis.

One such instance came not long after I devised this system of coping, when I was presented with the different chemo delivery options available to me. Given the time period, as well as where I was receiving my treatment, I had to decide between one of two choices. The first involved being hooked up to a drip and having the drugs administered intravenously. Should I decide on the second option, I would have to undergo surgery again, this time for the insertion of something known as a port. The port would be placed under my skin and would then be connected to an artery or a vein, and the drugs would be fed into my system this way. Neither method sounded like something I was eager to get going, but in the end I opted for meeting up with an IV bag every once in a while over the course of six months. I was told that the port, while not without its issues, might be the better choice, but I couldn't stomach the thought of having to go under the knife again so soon. The last time, they had taken something out of my body instead of inserting something, but I was nonetheless terrified that this operation would yield an equally terrifying outcome.

Once my choice was made, the time came for me to hear how, in spite of the fact that there is no perfect way of administering chemo, I had made the decision regarded as being the worst of the two. In the spirit of this, I was promptly informed that using this means of treatment meant that I would most likely experience issues with my veins for the rest of my natural life. Moreover, there was a whole host of things that could happen to my veins while I was still receiving treatment. Among these possible side effects was the potential collapse of my veins, meaning that they couldn't carry life-sustaining blood to parts of my body, as well as the infliction of severe damage to these structures and the vital organs they fuel as a result of pumping them full of drugs during each chemo session.

For all the potentially disastrous effects that my choice in administration could cause, I was determined to stick to my guns. Beings opened up for the port to be inserted was out of the question, so IV chemo was the only way to go. Apart from my aversion to having another surgery, my choice was also motivated by the hubris of youth I'd somehow managed to hold onto despite everything that had happened. I have to stress once again that I was 18 when I was diagnosed, and so my mind was still very much steeped in the sense of immortality, indestructability, and the effortlessness of life that most teenagers hold. I understood the risks associated with intravenous chemotherapy and knew that the use of this method could wreak havoc on my life. And yet, there was still a considerable part of my mind that shrugged all this off, responding to the list of potential side effects with that age-old adolescent catchphrase: "I can bounce back from this."

Looking back on the experience now, I understand all too well why I kept coming back to this arrogant phrase. Everything that lay ahead of me before I started treatment scared me more than I was willing to admit, and I couldn't even begin to fathom what my life would look like, should I be able to beat the cancer. Telling myself that I could recover no matter what was the light I was following to the other end of the tunnel. If you'd like a metaphor that sounds less like I was following the trail to the afterlife, think of that phrase like a carrot that was dangling in front of my face, and that I was chasing it with everything I had in me. Letting go of that and dealing with the reality of what could happen was absolutely out of the question. Giving in to that was more than I felt capable of, and accepting the fact that my future might not exist, let alone be uncertain, made my 18-year-old heart shake like it had never done before.

This prospect shook me more than I'd like to admit, mostly because the ideas and feelings I had about my future had always been under my control before. The way I looked at the road ahead was always something I'd managed to steer in the direction I wanted, regardless of what the picture itself looked like. Now, however, it was almost like I was being forced to choose one of two perspectives. The first, in which I gave in to the potentially bleak nature of my future, filled me with indescribable fear. And yet, I wasn't even that keen to accept the alternative, maybe because I wasn't all that sure the sentiment was all that genuine.

As much as I'd like to tell you that I overcame these emotional hurdles before my treatment started, I grappled with these fears and thoughts day in and day out during those six months. And however bad they were before, things became ten times worse when the chemo actually began. I was told from the beginning that the goal was to put me into remission, and that the form of chemotherapy I would be receiving was especially effective at making this happen. In order to do this, however, the cocktail of drugs I was being injected with would have to be particularly strong. And trust me, they were.

Outside of reporting the strength of the medication, there isn't very much I can tell you that would accurately describe what it felt like to undergo chemotherapy. Some days were better than others, though there weren't very many days that passed during which I wasn't crippled by pain. It made me sick, so much so that I didn't want to eat. I don't think I could have eaten, given how nauseous I constantly was. I vividly remember having a number of days when I desperately wished that I could just go back to the time when the only thing bothering me was the pain of the tumors in my chest. Yes, that pain sliced though me like a dagger, but every single sensation I experienced during that time paled in comparison to what that IV bag full of cancer cures made me feel.

Fortunately (I think), the chemo didn't cause whatever pain I was already feeling to be worsened. Though the nausea and lack of appetite were bad, I counted myself lucky that those daggering motions didn't become worse with every instance a drip was fixed to my arm. However, even that silver lining wasn't all that bright. While there was little pain added by the chemo, my internal environment was going haywire under the pressure and confusion caused by the cocktail of pills I was taking on a daily basis. Because the chemo produced the expected side effects, I was given several prescriptions, each of which was supposed to help ameliorate these effects. The thing is, whenever you take some form of medication, the chemicals of which aren't naturally found in your body, it's highly likely that there will be some more side effects heading your way.

While the meds certainly did help to lessen the severity with which the chemo affected my body, the nausea and lack of appetite caused by the treatment was soon replaced with a host of physiological consequences brought on by each of the other things I was taking. It's worth remembering that, at this point in time, I was not only receiving regular doses of aggressive chemotherapy, but was also swallowing prescription pills by the fistful. Whatever interaction the former medication had with my body's systems was changed and compounded by each tablet that subsequently entered my bloodstream.

In the interest of putting too fine a point on it, let me tell you about the friendly, neighborhood antinausea drug compazine. Compazine was, I suppose, meant to be one of the more effective drugs, given that the effects it was combating were being caused by regular rounds of cancer treatment. I'm not sure if it was the potency of the pill or the length of time I was on it (a couple of months, give or take), but one day my jaw decided to dislocate itself, all on its own accord. This particular side effect manifested in a matter of seconds, and I don't need to tell you, it took me completely by surprise. To give you an idea of what a suddenly-dislocated jaw looks like, imagine those demonic killer characters from horror movies, the type that look like they could swallow you and your soul in one simple, slack-jawed bite. To be fair, jaws that dislocate for other reasons might make you look the same, but I really only have my experience to use as reference.

In any case, I was horrified. My parents felt similarly when I presented my face to them, crying and screaming from the pain. Fortunately, they had the wherewithal to take me to hospital, a course of action I'm sure would have dawned on me much later had I been by myself, if only because of the shock brought on by the sensation of having my lower jaw seemingly separate itself from the rest of my skull. Dramatics aside, my parents took me to the hospital as quickly as they could. I can still vividly recall that car ride. My father sped through every light, regardless of its color, his hand never leaving the horn. My mother sat beside him, crying all the way, just as I was.

I remember speeding past one of the cars that nearly hit us as we barreled through an intersection and perceiving the horror of the other driver's gaze as he saw me. Luckily, things seemed to calm down not long after we got to the emergency room. I was given an injection containing the same ingredients found in Benadryl, albeit in a significantly higher dosage, and my face was more or less back to normal within about an hour.

# Two Years of Torture

As it turns out, those six months that marked the beginning of my encounter with cancer (dislocated jaw and all) were, in fact, just that, the beginning. The weeks dragged by, and every day started to bleed into the next, with the pain emanating from my heart soon growing to match the pain that shot throughout my body. Truth be told, I'm surprised by how well I remember those months, given how many different prescription medications were bouncing around my system. Regrettably, this cocktail of drugs wrought havoc on different parts of my body, my stomach in particular. Taking these medications meant that I was constantly nauseated, which eventually evolved into regular, heavy vomiting.

Now, as you may or may not know, cancer and the effects of its treatment tends to be somewhat unpredictable. So while I was taking the pills to help me with all the things my digestive system couldn't handle, my doctors thought it would be advisable for me to bump up my nutrition, which had been suffering due to the fact that I had lost all sense of appetite since the treatment started. Since I hardly ever wanted to eat, I didn't. Of course, not getting the requisite vitamins and minerals was further damaging a body that was already being put through the wringer in more ways than you can imagine. At my doctor's behest, I began taking prednisone, which I was told would help get my eating habits back on track. The prescription for prednisone, as effective as it was, turned out to be something more akin to an overcorrection than a return to the norm.

The list of things I could discuss when it comes to this particular drug is incredibly extensive, given the fact that I was on it for quite some time. In lieu of that, I'll give you the highlights, which essentially saw me develop an appetite that can only be described as ferocious. It was as though all the hunger I had missed in the preceding weeks came flooding back at once, and for every part of it that became satiated and removed from my system, another pang would stand ready to take its place. I ate more than I ever had before, gorging myself on as much food as was within my grasp. The trouble was that I remained ravenous no matter how much I consumed. Naturally, this took its toll on my body, and I soon became unrecognizable to myself.

The next domino to fall after this was tied more to my emotional state than that of my body. Nevertheless, with the two being as connected they are, the depression brought on by my diagnosis and treatment, as well as the myriad of pills and side effects, invaded every part of my mind, and soon started to slow me down physically, as well. When I reported this to my doctor, I was offered a solution with relative immediacy. And what else could this be but a prescription for another pharmaceutical aide. As reticent as I was to add yet another pill to my already-overloaded regimen, the heaviness in my head wasn't letting up any time soon, so I headed to the pharmacy once more.

Not to sound too morbid, but it seems appropriate, given my history with the substance, to use an alcohol-related metaphor to describe this experience. To me, it felt like I had walked into a bar and ordered a single whiskey. After drinking it, and asking the bartender for another, my request was rejected. He could see that I wasn't doing well, and what I really needed was a double, so a double he poured, and a double I drank. After that, the process was repeated, but given my ever-worsening state, he decided to change it from a double to a triple. Not long after downing this, the bartender informed me that the best course of action to ensure I had the best night possible was to serve me a cocktail. By this point, the six shots of whiskey I'd already imbibed did little to help my reasoning or arguing skills, so the cocktail was made and drunk, as per his recommendation.

Inebriated as I was by all the drugs that were fighting against the lymphoma, I was determined to make it through those six months. I knew little else about my life or about what my future would be, but I was entirely sure that there was nothing more crucial to my existence than getting through that half-year period of time and seeing 1995 rolling into 1996. All in all, this determination seemed to have paid off, because I did see the end of those six months, and the end of my chemotherapy course went to pass right along with it. Cliched as it may sound, I recall the final day of the sixth month coming to an end and feeling as if the weight of this ordeal was lifted off my shoulders. I knew that I wasn't entirely out from under Hodgkin's shadow, but I had come far enough to be able to see the light that lay beyond it. Consequently, when I went for a check-up scan a few months later, I was confident that the results would be what finally allowed me to take those last steps into the rays of the sun. Well, perhaps confident is too strong a word, but I was definitely hopeful. The scan, my doctor explained, would be used to determine whether the tumor had survived the chemo, or if it had been decimated, as expected. Once they had ascertained this, they could decide on what the next step would be, if there were any more steps to take. The particular type of cancer I had was regarded as highly treatable, and no one really suspected that there was any cause for concern. We'd followed the protocol, the only one that really existed for Stage IV Hodgkin's Lymphoma, to the letter. As such, both my doctor and I were hopeful that all the needles, nausea, and narcotics had been enough to do the trick. So I went for the scan, left, and tried my best to put it from my mind until the results came.

A few days passed before I got the call telling me that my scans were ready for collection. It struck me as being slightly odd that I was meant to pick up the scans myself, as I had assumed they would be delivered directly to my oncologist. It was a different time, I suppose, and I was entirely too anxious to find out whether the chemo had worked to stop and question the technician-patient-doctor courier system. As it happened, my anxiety was much too strong to control or ignore, possibly because I was considerably more sober now than I had been in a long time, and I knew there was no way I could make it all the way to the doctor's office without knowing what my future would be. All the information I needed to figure it out was in my hand, sealed in a large manila envelope. It wasn't until that envelope was given to me that I considered the weight of its contents, and this weight was far too heavy to bear for even one more moment. So, there in the parking lot of the technician's offices, I tore open the envelope and starting reading as fast as I could.

Now, I've never claimed to be well-versed in medical jargon, especially not at 19, so much of what was written down was like gibberish to me. However, I had spent enough time in hospitals, clinics, and cancer wards to pick up on a few key terms, some of which were used in the report. Unfortunately, I understood the more dire words along with the ones that would signify an end to this nightmare, and those that fit into the latter category were all but missing from those pages. While there was still much that my doctors would have to explain to me, I knew enough to understand that my cancer had come back. Additionally, I understood that the hell I had lived through for the better part of a year had ultimately amounted to nothing at all. And finally, I understood that the Hodgkin's lymphoma I had been diagnosed with was, in fact, the variation of the cancer that everyone was hoping I didn't have.

You see, when I was initially diagnosed, I was reassured that the chemo had an efficacy rate of approximately 95% and, as such, I was all but assured of entering remission once the treatment was completed. At the time, I hadn't thought to ask about the other 5%, probably because I didn't want the idea that I could be part of that percentile to pop into my head at all. As luck would have it, those check-up scans confirmed that I was indeed a member of that small, exclusive cancer club. At risk of making you jealous with just how low the acceptance rate into this group is, I have to tell you that only between 1% and 5% of people who are diagnosed with Hodgkin's lymphoma are found to have the variant that presents with this level of aggression.

The perks of membership were largely to do with the cancer itself, as it is extremely aggressive and does not respond to regimented chemotherapy, which is what I had been receiving. The realization of what this meant came flooding over me in an instant, and for a moment, my mind refused to keep going. Instead, it flew back through the past to that day in New York when the first set of scans were plastered against the wall. In painstaking detail, my mind forced me to relive every moment, from the revelation of the mass in my chest to the request by my doctor to perform open-heart surgery within less than 24 hours. Somewhere between hearing him ask me to make myself available for the operation and bursting into tears, I came back to myself where I sat in my car in a parking lot in Florida. Part of me yearned to do the same thing now as I had done then— to take off and run away to someone else's familiar, comforting embrace.

But I couldn't go. It wasn't just that I didn't know who there was to run to; it was that my body was incapable of doing anything but weeping. I sat in that parking lot for God knows how long, sobbing my heart out. The only difference between the tears that were falling now and those that fell in New York about a year before were that they weren't clouding my eyes. For some reason, they rolled right out of my eyes and down my cheeks, leaving my vision unobstructed. Because I could see, there was a part of my mind (the rational part, perhaps. Who knows?) that told me I was okay to drive, that I could handle the journey to the oncologist's office. And yet, despite this reassurance, my body refused. All the energy I had was being used to wring out my heart, to try and take away the effects of yet another salvo of some of the worst pain I'd ever felt.

My crying continued, and it was as if the salt contained in each tear was corroding all the ideas I'd had of what my life would be like after treatment. Soon enough, my future was the same empty, lifeless darkness it had been before. I knew nothing of what lay ahead. What I did know was that the bud of cancer that remained had started to blossom in my chest again, and this time its petals were made of lead, sitting atop a stalk made of indestructible iron. It was this knowledge that eventually led me, once the tears had more or less dried, to make the trip to see my oncologist. His reaction to the results was decidedly more clinical than mine, in that he managed to hold himself together. Being my doctor and all, he immediately began discussing options for treatment. I say "options," but there was in fact only one course of action that could be taken.

Surprisingly, I was informed that I would be receiving chemotherapy again. However, this time, it was a different type of chemo entirely, one that had been taken off the market and put out of use. The reason? It was killing too many of the patients who received it. I feel I should mention that this was not my doctor's description, but rather something I found out through research of my own. It was this same research that led me to discover that there was an acronym for the chemo I would be receiving: MOPP. In full, MOPP stood for Mustargen Oncovin Procarbazine Prednisone, which is really just the list of drugs mixed together and given to the patient. The "M" and the "O" were given intravenously, while the two Ps were presented in pill form. This is what's known as a combination chemotherapy regimen, the name of which is fairly self-explanatory.

For reference, the Mustargen used during MOPP treatments is otherwise referred to as "mustard nitrogen," which for a while was a key ingredient in rocket fuel, of all things. Moreover, the type of fuel formulated with Mustargen had been used in warfare, which I'm sure you can imagine inspired a great deal of confidence. Whatever feelings of trepidation I had before had been tripled when I learned this little tidbit, and yet there was nothing I could do about it. This was the only treatment that still had a chance of working, so rocket-fuel chemo it was.

Now, knowing what Mustargen was used for, I suppose that I shouldn't have been as surprised as I was when I received the first round of treatment, and it was worse than anything I could ever have imagined. In retrospect, it's possible that my experience was informed in part by psychosomatic issues. I knew how intense MOPP therapy could be, and through my research had determined the large number of dangers it posed to my body outside of attacking the cancer. In addition to this, the severity of my experience was exacerbated by one of my own choices, which was to continue receiving treatment intravenously.

Despite the agony I'd faced during the first round of chemo, I was determined to avoid surgery for as long as I could, and had yet again refused offers for the installation of a port. Because of this decision, every administration of the mustard nitrogen remains vividly etched into my mind decades later. A mixture landing somewhere between yellow and red, whenever the drug was placed into the drip, mustard nitrogen would produce an excruciating stinging effect that crippled me with its intensity. The best, most accurate description I can give you of what this felt like is that someone was pouring molten lava directly into my veins. From the moment it entered my body, it would start burning, and as the medication was absorbed into my blood stream, the stinging of the fire was carried throughout my entire body. I knew that it was meant to effectively burn away the tumors in my chest, but there was nothing you could tell me that would convince me the lava wasn't trying to eat away every single inch of my physical being.

I think undergoing MOPP therapy is about as close as any person can get to performing torture under protection of the law. I have to admit that none of the doctors, nurses, or technicians who tended to me looked as though they had any torturous intent, but I felt very much like the target of medical sadism with each round of drugs administered. This torture was set to continue for what was, I believe, between three and six months. However, despite being similar in duration,

MOPP was different from the previous chemo I'd received. Because of the medications' potency, I could only receive treatment a few times over the course of those months, and only after considerably longer intervals. Given how clearly I remember the intensity and the pain, you should have a good idea of just how aggressive this form of cancer treatment was. As expected, my body, which was still attempting to recover from those first six months, didn't react kindly to the presence of these new, violently powerful substances. It was only the second or third time I was receiving treatment that I started vomiting uncontrollably. However, because I wasn't able to stomach even the idea of eating, all that came up was bile that burned the back of my throat. Motivated by feelings of self-preservation (or perhaps just simple fear), I was very tempted to skip every MOPP session that came after. Naturally, that was out of the question. All I could do was grit my teeth and try to keep the flames from escaping my veins, as I was often sure they would. Eventually, the compulsion to flee from this torment died down, but it never went away, not entirely.

I'd like to say this desire to run away remained strong for a while, but there wasn't very much about me that was strong during those months. In fact, the worst blow yet came only a few days after the first time I became tempted to hotfoot it to somewhere in the world where I'd never have to hear the words "intravenous," "chemo," or "mustard" ever again. This time, the effects of the treatment didn't manifest gradually, but instead knocked me over with remarkable speed, making me incredibly weak. The weakness spread throughout my entire body, rendering me unable to walk or even get out of bed in the morning. I hadn't been told to expect this particular side effect, so I called my doctor as quickly as I could, asking him to help right the wrong I felt intuitively had arisen within my body. Sure enough, an appointment was made for the same day, one that I have memories of attending while also being entirely unable to remember how I got to his office. Somewhere in my mind, something tells me I must have driven there, as I always did. However, knowing how little I could do with my body, this still seems improbable to me. Nevertheless, under the haze of exhaustion and innumerable medications, I made it to the doctor's office and somehow ended up on his examination table. I'm sorry to disappoint, but the mystery of how I made the trip is yet to be solved, so we'll have to chalk this one up either to the intentional blocking out of certain events, or to the invention of the first driverless car—of course assuming that I had the wherewithal and materials to construct such a vehicle while undergoing cancer treatment in 1996.

Getting back to the topic at hand, the results of blood tests performed that day revealed that my physical weakness was the result of having become anemic, something for which I had to be admitted to hospital at that very moment. As it transpired, the level of white blood cells in my body had become dangerously low, thus my inability to do so much as hold up my hands. I assumed that, what with all the medical tools at their disposal and the relative commonness of anemia, I would be discharged within a matter of days. Yet again, wishful thinking got me nowhere. Had it been a regular case of anemia, they would have given me the requisite medication and sent me on my way as soon as my white blood cell count was back to normal. However, for that return to occur, your body has to be able to multiply the white blood cells it already has. Because of the strength of the MOPP therapy, coupled with the fact that I'd completed half a year's worth of chemo just months before, there were very few of these essential cells left. Those that had survived weren't nearly enough to get my body back to where it was supposed to be. The integrity of my circulatory system had worsened to such a degree that the only viable option was to undergo a blood transfusion.

Now, of course, given my religious history, blood transfusions had always been out of the question. However, I was over 18, unofficially no longer part of the church, and able to make my own decisions regarding my medical care. As much as all these factors would suggest that the choice was obvious, believe me when I say it was anything but. Remember that I was undergoing treatment in Florida, with my family (who were all still very much devoted to the teachings of the Jehovah's Witnesses) all around. Moreover, despite the fact that I had legally been an adult for the better part of two years, I still felt the pull of that innate desire to satisfy their wishes. All of this mulled around my head, compounded by my doctor's frankness when presenting me with my options. According to him, I had to choose between one of two things: a blood transfusion and death. Harsh as it may sound, hearing the reality of the situation spoken from another's mouth did help somewhat. Though it was by no means an easy choice, I decided that blood is thicker than water. (I understand that the real saying does, in fact, indicate *not* siding with your family, but my hands were tied.)

At the same time I was agonizing over transfusions and eternal damnation, my parents and other members of their religious community were working on finding their own solution to my medical problems. As it transpired, they had thrown themselves into research and had discovered that the white blood cell–depleting effects of the MOPP therapy could be ameliorated using intramuscular injections. One such injection had been developed specifically for the purpose of increasing the levels of these cells in the blood stream, thus alleviating symptoms of anemia while simultaneously reinforcing the immune system.

Naturally, since this in no way involved putting someone else's blood in my body, my parents tried as hard as they could to convince my doctors to opt for this course of treatment instead. As is often the case when a patient's parents start offering medical advice, there was some resistance from my doctors. In addition to this pushback, the insurance company was also unwilling to cover the costs of the injections. To them, financing this treatment after nearly a year of tests, medications, and intense cancer therapies wasn't worth the risk. I'd just about depleted all the funds I had, and I'm not altogether sure the insurance actually had the means to approve the use of the drugs, even if they wanted to. Blood transfusions were easier to access, more reliable, and much cheaper, so their rejection of the injection came with an urging to consider this option again. As we already know, this was out of the question. By this point, things had become much worse than before, and I wasn't awake long enough to be aware of what was happening around me. What I do recall is that tensions rose sharply after news of the rejection reached us. I'm not entirely sure if there were actual fights, but there wasn't much I could have done even if I'd been aware of them. What I do remember, however, is having moments of lucidity that lasted long enough for me to reaffirm my commitment to refusing the blood transfusion. Apart from this, the only thing I remember from those weeks is the feeling of finality that each reaffirmation elicited. The treatments that could save my life had been rejected, both by myself and by third parties; now all that was left for me to do was to accept that my life was coming to an end.

After a while, it seemed as though the people around me resigned themselves to the truth of the matter and began preparing for the end. My doctor, whom I suspect had been hoping for a different outcome, delivered a prognosis of about three months, four if I was lucky. The dark gloom of my impending doom settled over everything and everyone in my immediate environment, subsuming everything in its shadow of fear and heartbreak. What it didn't manage to conjure up, however, was feelings of fear. At least not in me. I was by no means excited to die. After all, I hadn't even made it into the second decade of my life.. Even so, I wasn't afraid of death. Perhaps it was the fact that I'd been put through hell trying to run away from it for the better part of two years that made me feel nothing more than acceptance that this was the end. Fleeing had made me exhausted in more ways than I could count, and I just couldn't do it anymore.

And then, just as soon as I had made my peace with entering the hereafter, news came that the shots had been approved, and I would be receiving the treatment after all. I think I was glad to hear this—I can't recall—but all I remember is thinking that this approval meant there was more pain to come. I had been told that getting the injection would be painful, but then again, there wasn't one part of me that hadn't been hurt by that point, so what was a few more rounds? In the end, that round was much more than I had expected. The injection itself was administered within minutes, but I remained within the confines of the hospital for several more weeks.

At the time, I resented this, but I understand now how important that observation period was. A lot of effort (and money) had gone into procuring this treatment, and making sure that it had been effective was paramount to determining the way forward. That being said, I certainly didn't enjoy those weeks in the hospital. As part of the observation, my blood had to be drawn and analyzed regularly. At one point, they were filling little vials between four and six times a day, with a nurse visiting me about every two hours to find a vein and prick me with the needle.

After the needle had been extracted for the last time, the sting became too much to bear, and I demanded to know why so much of my plasma was being taken. I was outraged. Had they not told me I needed new blood, more blood, just weeks ago? Now, here they were, taking out what little I had left. My anger, as misplaced as it may have been, did grant me a temporary reprieve, and they took fewer and fewer samples as the weeks went by.

Evidently, though they had less blood to work with, the results remained on a promising, upward trend. Time wore on, and my white blood cell count steadily grew larger. At the same time, the number of red blood cells in my system experienced a surge in numbers, and my circulatory systems was soon back in what can (generously) be described as fighting shape. And, as my blood grew stronger, so did my body. The weakness started to decline, and though I was by no means cured, I was significantly further from death's doorstep than I had been. Still, despite my improvement, I was only discharged when I starting insisting I go home. I can still recall the relief I felt when they told me they'd let me go, and I can still see the trip back into my parents' house clearly.

We walked up the driveway with my parents stationed on either side of me, holding up my body with theirs. We stayed like this making our way to my childhood bedroom, where I was gently deposited onto the mattress. All in all, I wasn't too thrilled with the idea of moving from one sickbed to another, but I made peace with the fact that this bed was at least familiar. Moreover, I knew that I was immunocompromised, meaning that the hospital was perhaps the safest place for me to stay, despite the risks being around other sick people presented. Being there could become lifesaving, should I need immediate medical attention. However, I also knew that being in my own home, surrounded by loved ones, would be just as good for me as any sterile environment could ever be.

Certainty and domestic longing aside, my journey with cancer continued, regardless of which bed I slept in. There were still a lot of drugs to take and a lot of treatment to undergo. Given recent setbacks, my doctors were still debating what exactly the remainder of this treatment would be. On the one hand, they considered sending me for radiation, which would last for another three to six months. Alternatively, I could undergo some tests and become a candidate for a bone-marrow transplant. The tests in question revolved around one key procedure: the extraction of a bone marrow sample. Sometimes called a "lumbar punch" because of the area of your back that they assault with the needle, the extraction is done while you're awake. They numb the area they work in, but you are still awake and present enough to see the sight of a very large needle being hammered into your side. After that, I was told, the marrow is sent off to the lab, where it's analyzed to see if the cancer has spread to this part of your bodily tissue. Thankfully, it hadn't, and I was subsequently declared suitable for the transplant.

I'm aware that it sounds odd to be dissatisfied about something like this, especially in light of the fact that I was dealing with Stage IV cancer, but I had my reasons. While waiting for the results, I had done some research, and the statistics regarding patients who made it through the transplant and patients who ended up in vegetative states had sent shivers down my spine. While there may have been a part of me that wished the test would have disqualified me from being eligible for a transplant, I was also relieved to learn that I still had options when it came to deciding the way forward. Still, there was one option I favored considerably more than the other. Though I hadn't been able to get my hands on a lot of information, the little I had been able to glean from the studies and articles meant I was entirely too afraid to opt for the transplant. As such, I somewhat happily informed my doctors that we would, in fact, not be moving forward with the procedure.

My happiness was short-lived, as avoiding the bone-marrow transplant meant that I was sent for radiation treatment instead. Now, before we delve any further into this section of my medical history, I'd like to share with you a small, illustrative tidbit. When referring me for treatment, the oncologist informed me that the severity of my cancer meant that I would be receiving the maximum dosage of radiation a person could receive in their lifetime. There was a legal limit, and my machine's dial was turned right up to it. This potency, apart from hopefully eradicating the cancer, would also prevent me from undergoing radiation treatment for the rest of my life.

They didn't tell me what would happen if I did happen to receive it again, but I've seen enough nuclear disaster movies to have a pretty good hunch. Tidbit aside, the radiation didn't feel as though it was doing very much—at least, not in the moment it was administered. I can't say that I liked it, but the fact that it didn't burn like hell going in puts it an inch above chemo in the hierarchy of cancer therapies. This pro was offset by the rather dark implications of one of radiation treatment's most significant cons. In the same instance my doctor warned me I'd be nearer to a nuclear plant than a human after the treatment course had been completed, he also let slip another warning: Because my body would be on the receiving end of some pretty strong radioactive rays, I was likely to experience issues with each vital organ contained in my chest—the part of my body where the rays were intended to do the most work. Just so we're all on the same page, this meant my heart, lungs, and thyroid would all possibly be affected. All things considered, this seemed to be something I could live with if it meant that I could, indeed, live. So I went along to all my radiation appointments, received the blast of rays for six consecutive months, lost most of my hair, then went home and anxiously awaited my next doctor's appointment when I would be told if all that effort had meant anything at all.

# Becoming the Victim

With the physical aspects of my cancer treatment now thoroughly explored, we're jumping back a bit to the first round of chemo I received. Now, to be perfectly honest with you, I haven't kept up with the trends in oncological treatment in the decades since I completed the last round of my own. Today's therapies may be very different, but as we've seen, those used in 1995 were unpleasant in a number of ways. On face value alone, I'm sure that the physical effects of this treatment seem more intense—or, at the very least, more visibly damaging. While that might be true, it's worth knowing that the emotional impact of chemotherapy is just as painful, if not even more so. You have to remember that, when that first intravenous dosage was given, I was barely an adult, having just turned 18 a few months before. To make matters worse, while it not only felt like I was losing out on a time in my life when I ought to be capitalizing on my youth (a time I'd never get back), the prospect of dealing with something as heavy as cancer at that age terrified me to my core. As my bravery shrank in the face of this illness, much of my mood made a similar immediate descent.

The depression I fell into during those initial six months of treatment was largely brought on my feelings of loss. Somehow, I had managed to make it to New York and take the first steps on the journey that would bring me to my dreams. More importantly, while there were still some secrets I had to keep from my family, my time in the city marked the first occasion I could live with a degree of authenticity. So much had happened in the few months I had been there, and I was determined not to let it all have been in vain. And yet, despite the convictions I initially had, there was nothing to be done. I was stuck in South Florida, relegated back to the confines of my childhood bedroom. To make matters worse, the reason for my return prevented me from doing the things I used to— the things that had allowed me to hold on to my sanity when the world wanted to rob me of it.

However, it must be said that not every aspect of my homecoming was bad—at least not entirely. Though the circumstances were less than ideal, one thing that remained unaffected by my diagnosis was my relationship with my parents. Before we go any further, I have to qualify that statement by saying that, of course, our parent-child relationship shifted. Given the severity of what we were dealing with, how could they not? So while not everything was exactly the same as it was, the key components of our bond managed to make it through the ordeal relatively unscathed. It wasn't lost on me that recent events were taking just as heavy a toll on them as they were on me. In fact, their emotional struggles were sometimes clearly displayed.

I remember my mother once telling me that she wished she was able to take my cancer and give it to herself. Neither her maternal love nor her devotion wavered, not even for a second. But as comforting as it was to know that she was as protective of me as ever, there was nothing anyone could do. So, although her desire seemed heartfelt (and slightly upsetting to think about), I would answer her with a simple "No, you don't," hoping that she would understand that nobody wants something like this. I told her as much, underscoring my point by informing her that no one deserves to go through this. In the moment, my words were sincere enough, but in the time that would follow, I couldn't help but wonder why it happened that *I* was deemed deserving. As illogical as this train of thought may seem in hindsight, it integrated itself all too easily into the malformed mindset under which I functioned at the time.

I had experienced difficulties with my parents' religion and the views that came with it for some time. Although I no longer frequented Kingdom Halls or counted myself as a Witness of Jehovah, I could still vividly remember what we had been taught was unacceptable, and what we had been advised was best left by the wayside. To the mind of an already distraught 18-year-old, there was nothing anyone could say or do to remove the idea of cancer being some kind of divine penalty from my head. As you can imagine, I couldn't shake the feeling that my sickness was God showing me just how he felt about people who thought, felt, and did the things I had done. However, as heavy a weight as this was to have lying on my heart, I couldn't give in to my sadness just yet. For the first few months of my treatment, I did my best to turn my attention to other things.

I had gotten a job at a local restaurant, and would try as hard as I could during shifts to concentrate on my work. I was determined to carry on as if nothing was wrong at all. I was happy to pretend that I had received no diagnostic news and that my insides were perfectly, youthfully healthy. My determination was offset somewhat by my boss, who always assured me I didn't have to come in whenever I was feeling sick. It wasn't exactly a five-star restaurant, and someone could easily fill in for me. Still, despite the ease with which he could make other arrangements, I appreciated his kindness. I also appreciated the fact that, as living with cancer goes, I was pretty lucky. I was fortunate enough to have a job, let alone one so flexible. On the personal side of things, I counted myself lucky to be able to leave the house and do something productive with my time. I appreciated that I could regularly put on other clothes, leave the house, and talk to people who weren't my parents.

Outside of my work at the restaurant, those early days didn't have too many good things going for them. I became upset quite easily, and would repeat the phrase "I'm sick and tired of being sick and tired" over and over again whenever my mood took a turn. Something similar would run through my mind every morning. When my eyes opened, my first thought was filled with something not unlike frustration thinking about how I had to deal with cancer, tumors, treatment tubes, and all their attached parts for yet another day. At some point near the end of the third of those first six months, my mind and my heart, which had both already been in precarious positions, took their steepest of dives to date. The depression that had lagged somewhere close behind me all this time finally caught up, and I found myself unable to fight the despondence that so desperately wanted to take over me. I began to cry, and there was a good while when I just didn't stop.

I wallowed in my despair, and, if I may say so, did this exceptionally well. On an almost daily basis, I would listen to every sad song I knew, sobbing out the lyrics along with the recorded voices. At one point or another, my father heard my melancholy accompaniment and asked whether I thought it was a good idea to listen to music that so closely reflected the nature of my internal state. Instead, he suggested, I should listen to something more uplifting. Truth be told, he wasn't wrong. Listening to those sad songs didn't make me feel better at all, but for some reason, I was content with that. I liked the fact that they didn't alleviate any of my pain. I didn't want that; all I wanted was to cry.

This desire stuck around for a while, becoming stronger whenever someone would offer their condolences or express some form of pity. Though every "I'm sorry" seemed sincere, I wasn't interested in any of it. I didn't want their apologies, I would inform them, nor did I want their pity. Apart from shedding a few tears now and again, I didn't really want very much at all. The only thing I did want was my life back. All I wanted was to live like I had before, to live in any other way than I was living at the time. Living like that wasn't something I was accustomed to, obviously. Still, however alien my new life was, I remained convinced that I had brought all of this on myself.

At no point was even a single blame-laden finger pointed in my direction, and still it seemed to me that I had strayed so far from the person my family, society, and even God himself had wanted me to be that this was some higher power's last resort at reeling me back into my place. Through all the crying and emotional heaviness, there was a part of me that still remembered that my life might get better some day. Granted, this part wasn't very large or very strong at that specific moment in time, but it was there nonetheless. Should the day ever come that I could be completely rid of cancer wards, treatments, and prescriptions, that part of myself would move to the front of my mind. Until then, however, there was only sadness, and there was only waiting.

Chapter 5:

# Consciousness Be Damned

As the 20th century started coming to a close, many things in my own life were similarly drawing to a close. In 1997, I turned 20, and in spite of the universe's best attempts, life went on. The time spent in cancer wards and doctors' offices also was soon drawing to a close, and in its place arose a new, exuberant lust for life. Of course, being 20 and newly released from the limitations of chronic illness, the world was mine for the taking. Unfortunately, moderation wasn't one of my strong suits in my youth.

## Internalizing Stigma and Hate

In 1997, nearly two full years after I began my first round of chemo, the last radiation sessions were conducted, and I was out of the woods—sort of. Though I was no longer being actively treated for cancer or anything caused by its presence in my body, I couldn't yet lay claim to anything resembling remission. For that to happen, half a decade would have to pass. That's to say, I'd have to make it a full five years without the cancer making an appearance again before I could join the club for people who were about as close to cured as you could get after having had cancer. Thankfully, I got the all-clear just two years into the new millennium. In 2002, at the ripe old age of 25, my oncologist declared that I was officially, properly, and legitimately, in remission. My journey with cancer had come to an end—at least for the foreseeable future—and you'd think that things would be smooth sailing from here on out. By this point, none of you should be shocked that it didn't turn out quite like that. Though one traumatic road had wound to its conclusion, I had long since embarked upon another. Of course, at the time, I had no idea things would progress as far as they did.

Way back in 1997, I did all I could to take advantage of the fact that I might be able to see my 21st birthday. The thing is, this taking-the-flower-by-the-thorns attitude grew to be a little too strong, and it stuck around for just a little too long, but more on that in a moment. In the interest of balance, I should mention that the period following the end of my cancer treatment did also include a return to higher education.

Though the first two years of this time were lived outside the walls of academia, I eventually made my way back to college in 1999, completing my undergraduate work in 2002. In the same year I received the news that I was in remission, I obtained a BA in theater with an emphasis on performance. Of course, my stint in upper education wasn't without its wild moments, but let's take things one step at a time.

# Self-Medicating

It was made patently clear to me from the time of my very first diagnosis that remission takes a while to achieve. Being deemed officially cancer-free was something I could only hope for, and it seemed to be an unlikely, unattainable abstraction for the longest time. However, when the second year of treatment came to an end, and there was no cause for immediate concern, all the patience I had was immediately lost. I'd already been through this once, and I was determined to live as much of my life as I could while waiting for the all-clear.

Truthfully, I had no idea if that news would ever come, and the idea that it might not terrified me. It was precisely because of this terror that my 20-year-old brain decided that cutting loose was the best thing to do. After all, death had been inches away a couple of times in the preceding months, and could very well be making its return in anything from a few weeks to mere days. So, while I had no idea what would happen in the future (if anything was going to happen at all), I had a myriad of ideas for what I could do in the precious present. Now, my first and primary aim was to recapture the years of my youth that had been stolen from me. All things being equal, I don't think this was a bad plan. The execution, however, could be considered less than ideal.

The first thing I did after receiving treatment was, in hindsight, an attempt to continue the curing process I was convinced I needed. One of the vices I had to give up after my diagnosis was alcohol, and in spite of the fact that I was still below the legal drinking age, I ran straight back to the bars, illegal license in hand. I was eager to readopt my tried-and-tested coping mechanism. I craved the numbing effects that I knew liquor would give me, and quickly made it a part of my regular routine. It wasn't long before it became evident that I was drinking to do much more than just relax.

Though I was oblivious to the fact that my alcohol use had become problematic almost immediately, I was fully aware that the liquor was being used as a tool. In the two years leading up to my return to the social scene, I had endured more trauma than I thought I would ever face in my life. And although I was surrounded by friends and family throughout the entire process, many of whom reassured me of the randomness of cancer's manifestation, I still felt as though what had happened to me was nothing more than a punitive measure. It was true that I had been enveloped in the love of my hometown, but I remained convinced that every tumor, test, biopsy, blood sample, radiation blast, and chemo injection was God's way of emphasizing his rejection of me.

This feeling extended beyond divine condemnation, leading me to continue believing that the people with whom I shared a home, a town, and even the streets I walked, regarded me as worthless and deserving of rejection and abandonment. Moreover, this feeling remained lodged in my heart regardless of how they actually treated me. This resoluteness stemmed from the fact that, as kind as people were to me, they still remained members of the same religious community that had first caused this perception of rejection and disgust to manifest. Every time someone spoke a kind word to me or showed me some measure of humanity, my mind would almost immediately remind me of the fact that they continued to engage in and uplift the very teachings that had taught me to hate myself. However hospitable they may have been, this continued dedication spoke for itself as far I was concerned.

Whatever my interpersonal circumstances were, to my mind, it was perfectly clear that I was despised by the world around me, and even though I knew that there were indeed people who loved me, there was nothing to be done. This certainty was immovable, and with every day that it remained lodged in my brain like a splinter, the more painful its presence became. Luckily, I knew something that could take that feeling away—along with all the others in my head. As I resumed the drinking habits I had cultivated in New York, there was a part of me that understood that talking about what I felt and thought might be a better, healthier solution.

However, every time this thought came up, it was swiftly drowned in the contents of whatever bottle was available. There was no way I could ever give voice to these awful thoughts, largely because it meant divulging other parts of my identity about which I felt equally ashamed. Sharing was not an option, nor was anything remotely resembling external expression. Once those had been eliminated, all that was left was the process of internalization. The only thing left to do was to stoke the flames of self-hatred that burned in my heart. Of course, the pain of the fire meant that I was fighting with myself quite often as different parts of me attempted to put out the flames or otherwise stoke them even higher.

# Just a Bit of Juice in College

Time went on, and my internalized hate continued to eat away at my heart, soul, mind, and just about every part of my body it could dig into. I'd already experienced similar sensations years before, but these were, fortunately, less medically concerning and more the result of societal concerns. Nevertheless, the pain was mounting every day, and as these things tend to go, I found after a while that the numbing effect of drinking was becoming less and less potent. As luck would have it, this wasn't the only habit I'd picked back up from my first days at college. Along with diving headlong into old drinking habits, I had also decided to restart my love-hate affair with cigarettes.

If you'll recall, there was no particular reason I started smoking when I was 18, and this was the case when I tried again at 20. I suppose it felt right to start smoking again, given that it had supplemented my alcoholic activities in the past. Moreover, smoking was something that was just done, by all appearances. My friends at the time all smoked, though many of them crossed over into realms beyond the fairly innocent nicotine that I decided to stick with. However, it's only a matter of time before you get bitten if you're always hanging out in the lion's den, and I soon found myself venturing into the same areas of exploration as my friends. There were a variety of substances available, as everyone was putting something different into their hand-rolled pipes. Of all the things on offer, I gravitated at first to the least strong inhalant I was given: the devil's lettuce.

Soon enough, marijuana became a key part of my regular substance rotation, forming the third leg of the tripod of inebriation upon which I rested the majority of daily functioning. Still, despite the fact that I was becoming increasingly reliant on the effects of alcohol, nicotine, and marijuana to help quiet the dark thoughts clouding my mind, I saw no reason to be concerned about my habits. Instead, I very much embraced the notion that, for some people, marijuana is a gateway drug, and I gradually became more closely acquainted with the other denizens of the world of illicit substances. The exploration of this world was helped in no small part by my introduction to the rave culture that dominated the latter half of the 1990s.

The scene, as it was known back in the day, was a mecca for all the habits that were borderline dangerous, intoxicating, and exciting. As the time I spent at raves became more frequent, the list of substances I used to help me live in the moment grew longer and longer. The first one I was aware of was ecstasy, the name of which I think tells you all you need to know about what this drug did to my mind. Ecstasy (among other things) soon became a staple of my partying routine, largely in the form of pills stamped with a variety of cartoons hailing from my childhood. Memorably, Batman pills were offered multiple times, and of course they were never refused. The cartoon pills were a great way to get high quickly. Their strength, coupled with everything I wanted to hide or forget, ensured that I never thought to ask what was in them when they were offered. After all, I reasoned, I hadn't entered the scene alone, but had come with friends, one of whom I'd known since high school. I was surrounded by familiar faces (most nights), so there was no reason to feel apprehensive. Besides, too many questions would have ruined the mood and likely alienated me from other people on the scene. I couldn't have that because heaven knows I needed as many distractions as possible, however dubious their origins may be.

I should say that I did eventually have the presence of mind to question what those pills were made of. With the help of the internet, I found out that my cartoon helpers were actually called "dirty" pills. The moniker was derived from the fact that they were laced with a variety of hard substances, including methamphetamines and heroin. In hindsight, ingesting them with the regularity and with as much gusto as I did was not the smartest thing to do. In all fairness, however, there was no part of me that wanted to know what I was taking during my time on the scene. Doing so would mean reckoning with reality, even just for a moment, and that was something I was absolutely determined not to do. Dodging the real world with such desperation was something I though of a lot, especially during the rave period of my life. One of the people who had introduced me to the scene was the aforementioned high-school friend, who was, in fact, an old girlfriend I had reconnected with. Though she was a wonderful person whose heavy presence on the scene contributed significantly to my education of rave culture, seeing her forced my mind back to the past.

We'd bump into each other every so often, and every time we did, her face served as a stark reminder of everything I was trying to change about myself.

# Just a Bit More in Grad School

Raves, weed, spirits, and cartoon character–embossed pills were the characteristic components of my undergraduate years. These habits endured even after I obtained my BA, when I started pursuing an MFA in motion-picture producing. At this point in time, I had been in remission for nearly a year but had been making the most of my time away from the cancer ward for about six years. For more than half a decade, substance use had been a regular part of my life, and I had no plans of stopping any time soon. As I reasoned, I had made it through all four years of undergrad without encountering any major issues related to my lifestyle. So, although I was now moving on to grad school, where the work was more intense and the stakes significantly higher, the fact that I'd made it through the preceding years unscathed signaled to me that I could keep things just the way they were.

This was the mindset with which I entered the first days of my master's degree. However, I didn't make it very far into the semester before my desire for overachievement kicked in. Regrettably, this desire didn't manifest as part of my commitment to my studies. Instead, it securely attached itself to my recreational habits. My party days were still in full swing, and illicit substances were still very readily available. Despite this, I had become something of a creature of habit near the end of the '90s, and stayed that way well into the 2000s. Now, however, I was in grad school, steadily making my way to the life I'd always wanted, and the sky was the limit. So, when harder drugs were suddenly and regularly on offer, I jumped from the outcropping I'd built out of alcohol, marijuana, and other party drugs and happily leapt further down the rabbit hole.

This is a very roundabout way of saying that I was introduced straight meth for the first time. For the uninitiated, taking "straight" meth means using the substance in its purest form. Where the pills passed out at raves were made from a mixture of different substances of various levels of potency and addictiveness, straight meth was taken as-is, with presumably no other drugs added to interfere with its effects. Meth was first offered to me by someone with whom I was "friends" at the time, though I use the term loosely.

The thing you have to understand about meth is that its potency is incredibly high, meaning that the drug can take over your life at an alarming rate. Though you don't immediately drop down to rock bottom, using meth even once or twice puts you on its fast-track. Interestingly, though I did begin using meth regularly, it was never more than a means to an end for me. My drug of choice had always been alcohol, and being a creature of habit, I stuck to what I knew. Any and everything else I smoked, snorted, or ingested was only ever intended to distract my mind and body from the drunkenness that had begun to set in. By getting high, I could go back to drinking quicker than if I waited to sober up. Under the influence of both drugs and alcohol, I could imbibe as much as I wanted to. And while I would feel the numbness I so deeply craved right there and then, I wouldn't have to deal with any of the substances' other effects until they had all worked their way out of my system, something I did my utmost best to ensure rarely happened.

Moving back to my academic exploits for a moment, we find what I considered at the time to be the greatest testament to the seeming lack of problems caused by my drinking and partying habits. Over the course of my graduate years, I made a thesis film, and was lucky enough to have my work receive some awards attention. With the state of my mind as it was back then, the logic according to which I operated justified my actions entirely. Yes, I was going out often and taking a number of different substances that, when mixed in a combination that was just slightly off, could prove to be fatal. But I had also managed to study for and obtain another degree while continuing these behaviors. Not only that, but the work I did was received well and was deemed to be of a high standard. When you put all of this together, you would find that there was absolutely no reason for anything to be altered at all, at least not to the twisted sense of understanding I employed at the time.

# Teaching and the Deleterious Cycle

We skip forward a bit now, to the time after my graduation in 2004. Not long after I obtained my MFA, I was appointed as an adjunct professor at a university in Florida. Teaching hadn't really been the plan, but I was working in the field I loved, and spent my working hours talking about the art of performance and filmmaking, the two things I had fallen head over heels for nearly a decade before. So, while it wasn't exactly the job of my dreams, I was more than content with the state of my professional life. The university where I was first hired as an adjunct professor was one of a few at which I would teach for a few hours a week, hoping to inspire the next generation of filmmaking creatives— the same generation I had plans to become part of.

I spent a while in this position, roaming from campus to campus each day, taking up temporary residence in lecture halls, doing my best to convey the majesty of the silver screen and its composite parts before packing up and moving on. Evidently, my teaching abilities were better than I had expected, and in less than a year's time I had managed to secure a position as a full-time professor. At the time, this job encapsulated everything I loved about the world of film, and I was over the moon at the prospect of being paid to spend hours on end talking about acting, screenwriting, and all the other key components that go into crafting works of art in this medium.

My job as a member of an academic staff, both in the adjunct as well as permanent capacities, afforded me with a sense of stability and consistency I hadn't experienced in years. Admittedly, the only thing in my life that had remained relatively reliable was the availability of drugs and alcohol, along with the regularity with which I used them. However, outside of this, most things had been shifting and changing on a regular basis. My first attempt at college was derailed relatively quickly, and was followed by a period that could only be described as tumultuous. The two years I spent as a free agent after the end of my cancer treatment could also hardly be categorized as stable or predictable.

The same can be said of my undergrad years, when every weekend and night out held a plethora of possibilities ranging from risky to just inches short of certain death. All things considered, academia had been the only thing I knew would remain more or less the same. Though the content of the different curricula changed as I moved from one year to another, the classroom remained an environment in which there were few surprises, if any. Now, I was standing on the other side of the lectern, but the feelings of constancy remained the same. Ironically, this spurred a desire for change within me.

When I first started teaching on an adjunct basis, I was pushing 30 and still partying like the worst 21-year-old you know. This was not lost on me, nor was the fact that I hadn't progressed nearly as far down the road of life as my agemates, and was yet to achieve many of milestones that had long since faded from the view of their rearview mirrors. As a side-note, I do wish to stress the fact that every person's path is different.

Some are able to follow the plans they've had for years, others make up the plan as they go along, and some people have no idea how to go about planning in the first place. For queer people especially, the phases of life begin and end at much different ages than for our straight counterparts. Even so, it felt very much to me that others my age (both queer and otherwise) had achieved much more than I had, something that was due in large part to the fact that their paths had been unobstructed. So I was determined to change, to rid myself of all my bad habits, and commit myself to a clean life lived in the pursuit of happiness, stability, and good living. Unfortunately, my life didn't take place in the last 10 minutes of a 2000s romcom, and things weren't all that easy to patch up.

The greatest challenge I faced was trying to stop drinking and using. I tried many times, and failed time and time again. Soon enough, the notion that quitting was impossible was slowly starting to creep its way into my mind. Eventually, this idea did indeed worm its way into my consciousness.

In the process, it had eaten away all the determination I had to turn things around. In its place, it had left a number of gaps, each one of which was filled by those old cravings that sent me back to the bottle, the pills, and the chemicals time after time.

# Hitting Rock Bottom

Thus far, though my issues with substance use have hopefully been portrayed in the harmful light they deserve, the effects of these problems on life have yet to be fully explored. Rest assured that I won't walk you through each and every one of the bad things drugs and alcohol did to me. There are a number of interesting stories to be told there, but I'll save them for the sequel. For all the damage wrought, there are three specific incidents I wish to highlight as a means of illustrating just how deep into the hole I had fallen. These three occurrences took place over a period of about 13 years, beginning in 1997, not long after my doctors informed that cancer therapies would be suspended as we waited for the official declaration of remission. Newly released from under the heavy weight of cancer, my quest to seize the day saw one of its earliest developments during a night out on the town.

Since moving back to Florida in 1995, I had gradually reconnected with some of my high school friends, and we'd managed to keep in touch between chemo sessions and biopsies. The night in question began with these same friends, more specifically with an invitation to join them at a club. At the time, I was still living at home, and as such had to inform my parents of any and all plans to go out. Of course, having so recently undergone intense medical treatments, they weren't particularly keen to sign off on this excursion. However, I refused to give in, even when I was asked to reconsider my decision light of recent life events. In the end, the only solution we were able to find was my mom going out with me and my friends. Years later, I would realize that my Jehovah's Witness mother suddenly asking to accompany me to a night club in the late '90s was an act of desperation on her part. Maybe she knew something I didn't, or maybe she just wanted to protect me. Since I refused to stay at home, she took it upon herself to make sure that I would make it through the night. I'm not sure what went through her head sitting under strobe lights that night, but I'd bet money that she never thought she'd end up in a place like that, much less with her fresh-out-the-cancer-ward son.

For many, having their mom chaperone them to a club at the age of 20 would rank among the most mortifying moments of their life. For me, however, there was no awkwardness or embarrassment to found in the night at all. In a ranking of the most memorable moments of my life, seeing my religious mother crammed into night club seats with a bunch of drunken kids the same age as her son skyrockets to one of the top spots every time the order is reassessed. In my version of things, the night was extremely fun. We drank, then we danced before drinking some more, a pattern we followed until the wee hours of the morning. At some point, shots arrived and were swiftly downed. After that, the night seemed to fly by even faster. Though I can't recall what time it was when my mom and I left, I remember the roads being empty, leading me to believe that we were deep into the night. In a display of extremely bad judgment, I got behind the wheel of my car and started the journey back home. Somewhere along the way, the car swerved, and I was swiftly pulled over by the police. Surprising no one, I was charged with driving under the influence and subsequently arrested. When I look back on that night now, and even in the moment itself, what bothers me most isn't the fact that I suddenly had a criminal record or even the arrest itself. What haunts me is the sight of my mother alone on an empty road in the middle of the night as I was driven away in the back of a police car. This was the first of the three dominoes to fall, and should have served as a warning, if not a deterrent. Unfortunately, my journey down the slippery slope was just beginning.

Jumping ahead a bit now, we move on to the year 2008, which we know to be a time when my alcohol and drug habits were in full, intoxicating swing. Eleven years had passed since my DUI, I had only just stepped into the role of college educator, and my efforts at betterment were off to a rocky start. Now, an important piece of information to have before we proceed is the fact that I was misdiagnosed with bipolar disorder during the late 2000s. Following the incorrect diagnosis, I was put on medication to help with the condition. Given the fact that I did not, in fact, have bipolar disorder (more on this revelation later on), you can imagine the havoc these pills wrought in my mind. Add on top of that the fact that the severity of my drinking habits had increased tenfold since the start of the new millennium, and suffice to say that the things I was putting in my body were not mixing well.

Consequently, the second domino in the sequence fell when I received my second DUI. This time around, however, things were much worse than a midnight swerve. Before being charged the second time, I crashed my car—a white Volkswagen Beetle convertible, which I adored, and which miraculously didn't have the top down at the time of the accident. The car rolled twice, injuring me severely and ensuring a swift dispatch to the hospital. There, I jolted awake, confused and extremely combative to the point where I had to be sedated and provided with a breathing tube. Later, I would be informed that my parents visited me while I was unconscious, and I can only imagine the distraught looks on their faces. Call me a coward, but I'm glad I wasn't awake for their visit. I think seeing their expressions would have broken me for good.

The third and final domino fell just two years later, right at the start of a new decade. Similar to the first two incidents, I once again received a DUI, this time also following a car crash. In the spirit of that timeless sports metaphor, I was out on the third strike. My license was revoked (again), I was placed under house arrest, and found myself the proud owner of a brand-new ankle bracelet.

By this point, my substance abuse was the worst it had ever been, and I had long ago lost any idea that I would be able to get clean and stop using. Because of the severity of my addiction, all my time, effort, and resources were put towards obtaining drugs and alcohol. Eventually, this resulted in me violating my house arrest, an offense for which I was sent to a halfway house where I was to undergo intensive therapy.

# An Incurable, but Manageable, Circumstance

I don't think anyone would accuse me of being hyperbolic when I say that 2008 was one of the worst years recorded in my own personal history thus far. By this point, my dabbling in the practices of alcohol and recreational drugs had evolved into full-blown addiction, though I remained adamant that I had everything under control. There was a part of me, one that existed in varying sizes and degrees of potency, that was all too aware of the fact that the reins of my life had long slipped out of my hands. Still, I refused to acknowledge the truth of my situation, opting instead to commit myself to the habits I had already worked so hard to cultivate.

How healthy these habits were was not something I concerned myself with. Their efficacy in helping me forget and escape had not waned, and so it stood to reason that their continued functionality was justification enough for keeping them as part my regular routine. As you can imagine, this type of logic didn't lead me to many positive, fruitful experiences. Soon enough, as I fell deeper and deeper into the grip of substances, my decision-making skills were all but shot. I knew that what I was doing was bringing more harm than good into my life, and yet I found myself returning to the bottle and the chemicals time after time. I tried to pretend that things were fine, hiding the things I took from those in my life, and using wherever was convenient, and where I thought no one's eyes would reach me. As time wore on and my judgment deteriorated even further, I sought even more expansive escapism, and began spending my nights with people I had never met before, and who I would never see again.

These encounters were transactional in nature. Both of us needed something from the other. Whatever relationship existed between me and each of these people began when we first met, and ended as soon as each of us had our fill. Every new person I met provided me with an opportunity to have some fun without thinking too much. Regrettably, when you don't think too much, crucial things like protection tend to slip your mind as well. In the interest of being thorough, I should say that there were a number of protections that fell away during this time, or at least that were altered by my continued issues with substance abuse. One such protection was tied to my family, who had remained as strong as humanly possible throughout this entire ordeal. Despite how well I sometimes managed to convince myself I could hide my drug and alcohol use, they were all too aware of what was going on. While they may not have been privy to each detail or consequence of my addiction, they could see enough to know that things weren't going well.

Today, with the benefit of sobriety, I understand that I hurt them deeply, and my actions during that time will always remain one of my deepest regrets. And yet, no matter how much I put them through, my family's love never wavered. If it's possible, the protection and support they lent me in this time deepened, perhaps in an attempt to keep me safe from the perils of the world I had entered. If I'm being realistic, it was probably to keep me safe from myself. Although their decision to distance themselves from me (should they ever have decided to take such a step) would more than likely have been justified, they always allowed me to come home to them, and showed me nothing but love every time I came stumbling back from a night out on the town. My family demonstrated exceptional patience and thoughtfulness during this time, something I'm sure I never could have managed, had the roles been reversed.

Whatever the reason for their dedication, they stayed by my side the entire time, something that caused them a lot of pain; I couldn't see this pain at the time, and even if I had, I can't say that my mind would have been sharp enough to comprehend it or change my ways. I remember my mother trying her best to get through to me, telling me that she was losing sleep whenever I went out for the evening, or was missing for a few nights in a row. Despite how torturous this experience was, night in and night out, she never pushed me or gave me an ultimatum regarding my behavior. All she wanted, she assured me, was for me to live. For what it was worth, my father wanted the same. I don't believe either one of them expected me to cloister myself, but they wanted me to be safe, and to take better care of myself than I was. Unfortunately, their appeals fell on deaf ears. I was so deep in the hole at that point that changing my ways would require a lot of effort and work, neither of which I felt up to back then.

My brother's disposition during those years was different from that of our parents, if only slightly. In the way that only siblings can, he saw straight through me from the start. By 2008, when things had gotten this bad, he was more than a little fed up with me and my antics. However, this was the only way in which he differed from my mother and father. Apart from his annoyance, he constantly provided me with love and support, and remained a consistently positive presence in my life. Just like my parents, he was concerned and wished for me to do what would be in my best, healthiest interest. Now, admittedly, given the last impression I left you with about our sibling relationship, it may come as something of a surprise to hear about such profound levels of compassion and investment on my brother's part. As it turns out, my brother and I are much better suited to getting along as adults than we ever were as kids. Although there had always been love between us (we're family, after all), we had grown much closer during the period of my cancer treatment. I can't say that our relationship is entirely perfect—which sibling connection is?—but things have changed a lot since the days of animosity and annoyance. Perhaps because of this surge in affection, or perhaps because he had cared deeply all along, my brother was very worried about my drinking and drug habits. He wanted me to stop and knew that one of the best ways to do so ways to let me know that he wouldn't tolerate my continued intoxication.

One memorable instance of this took place during the period of time in which I had messed up enough to have run into some issues regarding my license and my legal commandeering of motor vehicles, which had come under scrutiny on more than one occasion. Put plainly, I wasn't allowed to drive. As a result, I asked my brother to come pick me up so the two of us could go and hang out together somewhere. Though I've long since forgotten what exactly it was we agreed to do (something in my mind compels me to say we would've gone out to lunch, but it's all pretty much guesswork at this point), I vividly recall his reaction when I opened the door for him. Unbeknownst to me, I was visibly intoxicated, which he of course noticed the moment he laid eyes on me. As is to be expected, he remarked on my drunkenness immediately. His statement was followed by a curt, simple "I'm leaving" before he was gone. The entire interaction lasted about 20 seconds, and none of it upset me, surprisingly. I felt his response was appropriate given the fact that, yes, I was drunk and no, I hadn't told him I'd been drinking. While I wasn't upset, I was surprised; not at my brother but at myself. Clearly, I was aware that I was drunk. What I didn't know, however, was how obvious my inebriation had become. In my mind, my buzz wasn't nearly strong enough to catch someone's eye, which clearly wasn't true. Somewhere in my mind, something told me that if things had progressed to the point where my drunkenness could be picked up immediately and on sight alone, my problem had become worse than I had allowed myself to believe.

This initial realization soon grew into certainty which itself evolved into a much louder, more constant thought in my head. Eventually, it dawned on me that something had to be done. I still had no intention of quitting, nor indeed any idea of how I would even go about trying to do so, but the reality of my physical state managed to push through the clouds obfuscating my mind. It became clear to me that I should at least make an effort to start looking after my health. To this day, I'm not sure what compelled me to seek out STI and blood tests—maybe it was intuition, maybe my guardian angel had finally managed to get a word in edgewise—but that was the first thing I decided to ask for when making an appointment with the doctor. All I knew was that this was where I could find something that should be addressed. Fortunately, I still had access to the same doctor I had seen when I was younger, and who was willing to see me and relay the test results. The day of that particular appointment is one I will remember for the rest of my life.

Because of my run-ins with the law and lack of a driver's license, my brother was kind enough to take me to the see the doctor. The journey itself was easy enough, as was the checking-in process. The difficulty began not long after, when I was asked if I would like a copy of my blood work. Naturally, I said yes, and was promptly handed a few sheets of paper with some freshly printed data on it. Before I had the chance to see what was happening inside my body, the nurse called me in. In the rush to make it into the observation room, I left the results lying on a chair in the waiting room.

When I realized my error, I offered to go fetch the paper, but the doctor gently refused, asking me to sit down instead. As I did so, he informed me that there was something he had to tell me. This alone made me nervous. I had known this doctor since I was a child and had never heard him use this tone of voice before, regardless of the severity of a diagnosis or prognosis he had to deliver. It wasn't that he was overly serious or even grave, but that he delivered the news rather dryly with a sort of matter-of-factness to his speech. There was next to no feeling in his voice, and his words were devoid of anything resembling emotive language. This was the language of a clinician, the same language that promptly informed me that I had HIV. Not only that, he said, but my viral load had become extremely high, which meant that the initialization of a medication regimen was an immediate necessity.

That was the last thing I heard before my mind caved in on itself, causing my awareness to retreat deep within myself. The doctor carried on speaking, but none of it made its way into my memory. I can't even say that his words were blocked out by my own racing thoughts or heightened emotional state. In fact, there was very little going on inside my head, potentially due to the internal cave-in that had happened only moments before. There were no feelings poking through the rubble of my mind; not sadness, not shock, not even confusion or denial. The only thing that managed to make it through was a brief flash of thought telling me that I had done this to myself, that I had been careless, and that this was the fate I deserved. Much later, my internal state would more or less compose itself back into what it was before, and I would be able to process things logically and carefully. In that moment, however, there was only the rubble and that self-condemning flash.

Sometime later, the appointment was over, the results had been delivered, and I was released back into the waiting room. There, I found my brother gazing at me with a concerned look on his face. He held the freshly printed sheet in his hands. I had known him all my life, which was enough time for me to know exactly what was running through his mind. We didn't have a long-winded, teary conversation. We didn't even react all that much. "You know" was all I could think to say. He met my statement with three simple words: "Yes, I know." The interaction ended there. A little while later we were in his car again, heading back home, back to our lives. I couldn't tell you what was going through my head in the time following my diagnosis. Not because I was numb to it all, but because my mind was a mess of chaos and confusion. I had been to hell and back, and the journey had made me come to the place where I now sat, the disastrous consequences of my actions strewn all around me—and in me, for all it mattered.

Yet, as bad as I understood things to be, I still couldn't bring myself to be shocked. From the moment my doctor spoke those words I felt as though he was just informing me of the manifestation of something I had believed all along was an inevitability. Does this mean I went into those situations expecting to contract HIV?

Of course not. But I knew that there would one day be a price to pay for my recklessness, and the universe had come to collect. I also knew that I was stuck in a cycle that would become more and more deleterious the longer I allowed it to turn. Sort of like the world's worst merry-go-round. I had no idea what I would do to make it stop, but I knew enough to know that I had to do something. I would try everything I could, as long as I did, in fact, try.

# The Ultimatum

At the end of this chapter, this part of the story concludes right as a new decade begins. Remember that third DUI I received in 2010? More importantly, remember the house arrest I was placed under and subsequently violated? As you will also recall, I was sent to a halfway house after this violation. There, the next of many concerted attempts was made to help loosen the grip substances had on me. However, my brain had already firmly nestled itself in a certain behavioral pattern, and it wasn't very long before the rules of this halfway house were also disregarded. This time, however, the consequences were severely different. I had now received multiple warnings, as well as three separate indictments for driving under the influence. After this latest offense, there was no recourse that allowed me to keep my life going the way it had been.

This period of bad choices began with that third DUI, which saw me outfitted with a snappy ankle monitor and the restriction of being under house arrest. This was approximately a year after my diagnosis, and I had an increasingly harder time keeping hold of the part of me that wanted to change for the better. As a result, I found myself sliding further and further downhill. My descent eventually lent itself to a change in my mindset. Since it didn't seem that I would actually succeed in my attempts at betterment, I might as well give in and embrace all the bad things to which I found myself drawn. If I couldn't make myself better, I would do my damnedest to make myself worse. I had attempted to turn things around in the past, and every time had ended up being a failure. Maybe, I thought, this was actually what my life was meant to be like; what I was meant to be like.

However, as strong as my conviction to fall further was, the world had other ideas. My actions didn't occur in a vacuum, and punishment after punishment was handed down, with each one being more severe than the last. By the time I was placed under house arrest, there was no stopping me, and I violated the terms of this sentence fairly quickly. As a result, I was sent to a halfway house with the expectation that I would cease my use of drugs and alcohol. To be fair, this wasn't a random idea or some blind hope someone had. I was required to stop using substances as part of the terms of my move to the halfway house. Naturally, and this will come as a shock to you, I paid very little mind to these terms, if any at all. I continued to get drunk and high, something that didn't go unnoticed by those in charge. One day, not long after my arrival at the house, I was pulled into the office of the pre-trial officer who was acting as the overseer for my case.

On this particular day, her manager was with her in the office. Not one to mince words, my officer asked me a question no one ever had, and one I'll likely never forget: "Joshua, do you want to be incarcerated?" I don't think she was trying to get a rise out of me, or even to scare me into submission. I think she was asking me genuinely, perhaps sensing the sense of resignation I held in my heart. Though my response to her question was negative, I couldn't help but regard the possibility of going to prison as yet another inevitability that had come my way. I hadn't resigned myself entirely, but the prospect of incarceration seemed to me to also potentially be an easier route to take. The alternative was a return to the fight for sobriety I had initiated, and lost, so many times before. The idea of being sober, of being free from the awful weight of drug and alcohol addiction was as much an abstraction to me as it was a reality for so many others. It seemed so far away, as if it existed in a place that was entirely unreachable, at least for me.

In any event, the ultimatum issued that day would come to life as my ultimate destiny. I left that day and returned to the halfway house, knowing that something was coming. Sure enough, there was a knock on the door only a few days later. In front of it stood the clinician in charge of the house, side-by-side with a police officer. The latter was brandishing a piece of paper: the warrant for my arrest. In the most perfunctory of ways, I was cuffed and taken away to meet the fate I had known was waiting for me. All other options short of death had been exhausted, so the judge's gavel came down, and I was sentenced to 18 months in prison. So much had happened in the years leading up to this, and yet in that moment, it all seemed to be so clear and so simple to me. This was my just desserts.

It was my comeuppance for all the horrible things I had done, and for the horrible, inherently awful person I was. There was no part of me that looked forward to what lay ahead, but at the very least, I understood how this turn of events had come about. More than that, I had expected it. Now that it was here, there was nothing to do but accept reality. Maybe (hopefully) there would be a point down the line where my fortunes would turn. For now, however, I wasn't going to hold out hope.

# Chapter 6:

# Seventy Men in One Room

The 2010s were a time of monumental change. The shifts taking place during this decade extended their reach to just about every corner of society. On a smaller, more personal scale, this period of time was equally as transformative for me. Though the decade did by no means start on a high, the ensuing years and all the experiences they contained affected me in more ways than I could possibly have imagined. By the time this part of my life came to an end, the person I had been before was nearly unrecognizable to me. Of course, the road that led me to that point was anything but easy. The journey was long, circuitous, and involved some of the hardest work I've ever had to do. And, as rewarding as my new life in that final destination has been, the first steps I walked on this path were some of the most unstable strides I'd ever taken.

## Entering Another World Naked

As much as I'd like to recount this part of my life as being an incredible time of rediscovery and rebirth, the truth of the matter is that these experiences only occurred relatively close to the end of my time in prison. The start of my incarceration was much, much different. It did include a rebirth of sorts, albeit one that was much closer in execution to my actual birth than anything else. After the sentence had been handed down and I was remanded in custody, I was taken to the South Florida Reception Center, where I would begin serving my time. Crucially, the word "reception" in the institute's name should be taken in the most literal of senses. The officers and other officials there had no intention of welcoming me to the carceral system (not that I'd expected warmth and hospitality, given that this was prison). Instead, they were there to take receipt of me like I was a particularly inconvenient package, the delivery of which they'd had to rearrange some of their affairs for. Before making my way there, I was shackled and loaded onto a bus with my fellow offenders. I knew nothing of them, and they knew nothing of me, but it felt remarkably like we were something akin to an army troop, sent to meet the enemy combatants (or wardens, in this case) who were waiting for us on the front, weapons at the ready.

Arriving at the reception center, we were greeted angrily by a sergeant. Note that when I say "greeted," the term is used both generously and loosely. We all filed off the bus before being made to line up again before entering the building. Our shackles clinked as we walked, the prison building that would be my home for the foreseeable future looming large in front of me. Inside, the rebirthing process began, and it was just as painful the second time around. Given the fact that I was able to recall the events taking place during this birth, it's possible that it may well overtake the first one in terms of pain, suffering, and humiliation. I was unceremoniously stripped of my clothes so I could be hosed down. Standing there against the wall, water blasting at me with worrying ferocity, I couldn't help but feel as though they were trying to scrub away the part of me that was still linked to the outside world. I understood the practical considerations of the practice, but nevertheless felt like part of me had been lost as my own scent, the one I'd lived with and used day after day, was wiped away and replaced with the same state-funded stench that the other prisoners reeked of. As you can imagine, dignity went along with the clothes. I don't recall ever being more self-conscious than I was in that moment. This feeling had less to do with comparisons and inadequacy, as it might under normal circumstances. In that moment, I had been made undignified by the nameless entities barking orders and corralling us like sheep. I couldn't have cared less about the naked men surrounding me. It was the eyes of those unseen authority figures, staring at us as their pupils dripped with contempt and superiority, that made me feel less human than I ever had before.

Another memorable event occurred on my first day in prison. Though we were by no means the same, at least not as it pertained to anything real or material, I was forced to become a nameless entity as well. My name was stripped away with my clothes and humanity, and we were made unrecognizable, becoming nondescript components of their punitive system. I hadn't thought I'd hold on to very much in prison, but I had at the very least expected that my name would remain in my possession. Though so many things were lost that day, one thing I gained was my first bit of insight into what an incarcerated life would look like. This glimpse was afforded me by the guards and prison officials who were in charge of our induction into the reception center. Within minutes of our arrival, we were disabused of any notions that we might be treated gently or indeed with any humanity at all. The first of many beatings took place before we had even made it to our cells, letting all of the inmates present know what lay in store for us down the road. Fortunately, I was spared the rod during that initial welcome to the prison system. Although more personal experiences would follow later, that first instance of violence certainly left an impression.

The rest of that first day was spent learning about the penitentiary itself and its inmates, as well as the schedules each of us were made to follow. Meals were served at set times, a curfew was in effect, and we would be granted access to fresh air through forays into the yard at specific times only. Outside of these designated activities, we were confined to our cells, forced to spend time with the cellmates we were introduced to not long after that initial hosing.

Although I was instructed to follow the same routine as all other prisoners, there was a special activity added to my roster, one that was reserved for others who, like me, had committed their infractions under the influence of things that were perhaps less than legal. Because I'd been incarcerated for violating the rules of a DUI sentencing, I had to submit to regular drug testing to ensure that I had well and truly kicked the habit. More pertinently, the testing was the closest thing the prison system had to a recovery program. Outside of this, I was expected to just quit substance use cold turkey.

# You Don't Belong Here

Acclimating to life behind bars isn't something that happens easily, but it is something that happens quickly. As disorienting as those first moments were, and as daunting as the prospect of being kept within the same walls for more than a year was, there was no time to get settled in. Adapting to the hierarchies, castes, and other pseudosocietal systems was a matter of survival. If you didn't get in line, and do it fast, someone was bound to help you to your place. This counted for both inmates as well as prison officials, with the latter often being the quickest and most eager to ensure the prisoners' submission. Understanding that compliance would be my best shot at making it through, I kept my head down and did what I could to see the end of each day. Soon enough, however, my name was called, and an issue was raised. Someone from the correctional services had noticed my diagnosis of bipolar disorder.

Given the severity of the condition, I was unable to remain among the general prison populace. Out of concerns for safety—both theirs as well as mine—I was moved to a separate camp within the penitentiary. Specially constructed and equipped for inmates dealing with issues related to mental health, my transfer disrupted the process of acclimation in which I had begun to make progress. Now, I was in a brand-new environment, surrounded by brand new people who followed different rules when interacting with one another, and who were regarded in a much different light than the rest of the prison's inhabitants. This isn't to say that life was any better in this camp, as the guards' gaze was still very, very far from kind.

Moving meant starting the learning process from scratch, this much I knew. Little did I know the extent of the education I would undergo after my transfer. You see, becoming a resident there was the first of two significant changes I would experience in quick succession. The second was slightly more impactful, at least in terms of how I understood myself, my mind, and the way in which it viewed the world. Because the camp was designed to help with the treatment of psychological disorders, evaluations and therapy sessions were added to the roster of regular activities. It was through this regular consultation with mental health professional that I came to learn that my diagnosis had been made in error. Consequently, I was adversely affected by the drugs I had been prescribed, as they had entered my system and gone to work "curing" a condition that had never been there in the first place.

At the same time this was happening, other changes kept coming one after the other. Since my arrival in the new camp, I had become acquainted with some of the other prisoners and had even started forging relationships of sorts. Unfortunately, mingling with the others wasn't something I was motivated to do by a desire to make lifelong friendships. Instead, I wanted to avoid becoming isolated from the others. Isolation meant that you had no one in your corner. More practically speaking, this meant you had no one to intercede or maybe help you, should a target be placed on your back. A lack of connections was a lack of security, and it all but ensured that you would be abused or exploited at one point or another. This was the way things went, and though it was ultimately every man for himself, there remained strength to be gained in numbers higher than one.

Through my foray into the social ranks of Dade Correctional Institute, I met a number of people. I wouldn't remain in contact with them for the entirety of my sentence, but each of them would inform and influence my experience of the following months to greater extents than I could have imagined. This cast of characters (whose names have been altered in the interest of privacy) included Flaco, an impressively tall Latino man with whom I became friends under the impression that he cared about me and my well-being. Next was Martin, an older Black man who intimidated me to no end when we were first introduced. As I got to know Martin, it transpired that while he was certainly one of the big dogs, he consisted of a considerable quantity of bark, yet possessed no bite.

Also older than me was Robert, the first murderer I ever met. I encourage your opinion of Robert not to be colored by his crime too much, as he regularly expressed his regret and experienced symptoms of depression brought on by his actions. Another member of the Caucasian persuasion was Steve, a White supremacist who, despite his firmness (and regrettable racial views), was surprisingly kind to those around him. It will shock you to learn that Steve was kind even to the likes of me. Rest assured that this was just as much a surprise to me as it may be to you. Finally, there was

Michael. For now, all you need to know about Michael is that he was from another building inside the camp.

My move to the new camp was followed by the confirmation of a suspicion that many of us had held for quite some time. Though none of us knew exactly how, it seemed that the guards knew a lot about each one of us, or at the very least had easy access to resources that provided details of our lives. This meant that my educational background had at one point or another become known to the prison authorities. While my possession of an MFA would only later come into play, the fact that I had achieved this level of education already made me appear different in the eyes of the guards. This altered perception was compounded throughout my time there as I was moved from department to department, answering questions and putting my signature on various documentation, the contents of which I'm still unclear on.

Throughout this entire process, the same phrase would be echoed in my direction time and time again. Nearly everywhere I went, I would be told that I didn't belong there. At the time, this was refreshing to hear, and I still appreciate the sentiment to this day. Actually, I appreciated the confirmation I was able to get because of the sentiment. But by no means did I feel that I wasn't supposed to be there. After all, I had committed the crimes for which I'd been sentenced. In that regard, I was no different from anyone else in the prison. What I felt whenever I was told that my presence there was in error was the affirmation that this entire experience was a test, one I not only had to survive, but also one I had to use as an opportunity for growth. The life I led in the time leading up to my incarceration wasn't sustainable, nor were any of the activities or habits I had used to populate my waking hours. This was my chance to break the cycle, and it was up to me to ensure that, when I left, it had well and truly been undone.

## Another Chance to Teach

Not long after the misdiagnosis was undone, I was called out from the crowd again. Things were changing again. This time, however, I was set to remain in the same place, albeit in a different capacity than before. Because of my past experience in teaching, my work assignment for the duration of my sentence was to function as an educator for my fellow inmates. In the past, I hadn't been sure if a life in academia was for me, but given how confusing the preceding years had been, I was happy that this appointment gave me a chance to return to something that was familiar to me, more or less. This happiness was accompanied by a healthy dose of nerves and, if I'm being honest, fear. Before, I was in charge of teaching a subject I loved, and my students had been college students, most of whom were a good few years my junior. This time around, I was plunked in front of a white board with a number of strangers all looking at me, ready to learn about none of the things I had studied. Some of them were around my age, many of them were older, and none of them formed part of what I would describe as my "educational comfort zone." In spite of this, I had a job to do, and as intimidated as I was, these men deserved the same chance at an education that I had been so generously afforded more than once. I feel compelled to mention that my confidence in my teaching abilities was bolstered somewhat by the fact that I was mainly preparing my inmate-students for the exams that would get them their GEDs. Also, I should point out that my area of expertise mattered little to those who appointed me to the position of teacher. To them, just the fact that I had an MFA meant that I had spent enough time in classrooms to manage the set curriculum.

So it became my mission to fulfill my responsibility as teacher to the best of my abilities, and as time went by, and facing the men became easier and easier, it appeared that there was a kind of symbiosis developing among us. With every lesson taught, I felt that I understood them better. Slowly but surely we began to learn about one another, and while I can't say that I grew very close with many of them, the bonds we were able to forge were enough to cut through the haze that settles over your mind in a place like that. With clearer eyes, it's much easier to see another person's humanity. Moreover, by seeing others in a more illuminating light, your understanding of yourself grows. So, the longer I taught, the more I felt I was approaching something that could be considered a coherent sense of self.

Of course, within the realm of detention that runs parallel to our own, nothing is ever simply what it appears to be on the surface. In this instance, fortunately, what grew from the interactions between me and my pupils was much less insidious than other developments that had manifested throughout my sentence. Although none of us were friends, exactly, all of us were connected to one another through our regular interactions in the classroom. Subsequently, this meant that I grew less and less isolated from the other inmates. Had I remained wary of the general prison populace, I may as well have started painting a bullseye on my back. Luckily, I now had a role to play and a specific space into which I could be slotted on the totem pole. Additionally, as is the nature of symbiosis, I gave as much as I got, helping those who pursued knowledge to obtain it. While I can't say with any confidence that this was an equal exchange, each party involved seemed to have achieved a happy medium when it came to getting by. This medium involved regular recalibration on my part, both of my approach to teaching as well as my general communication skills. Each change I made was intended to avoid making one of my students upset, regardless of any actual connection I had to the reason why they would feel bad. Though this wouldn't last, it was instrumental in getting me through those first months which, in hindsight, were perhaps the easiest of all.

# Being the Best at Bad Doesn't Work

As you can imagine, serving a prison sentence of any length tends to be pretty demoralizing. Spending day after day staring at the same walls, following the same routine, and going through the same motions takes its toll on your heart and mind. For many, their days were filled with nothing else, and they were simply biding their time until they became eligible for parole, their sentence ran out, or they died. While I couldn't exactly fill my time with the things I'd like to do, being in prison and all, there was a bright spot that would pop up every so often, reminding me that there was life beyond the bars and the yard. This sliver of light was, of course, my family, who would come to visit me regularly, checking up on my well-being while also delivering news from the world I had so recently been a part of. Initially, it hurt to see them there under the harsh light of fluorescent prison bulbs. Though they never said a word, I'm sure it pained them to see me in that place. Fortunately, for want of a better term, we were never separated by thick layers of plexiglass. In the institution where I was detained, visitors and inmates were allowed to sit together in a common room while being closely watched by a number of guards. There was some leniency when it came to visitation, as we were allowed to give one hug or kiss to the people who came to see us, both when they first sat down as well as when they said their goodbyes. However, these exchanges had to be quick, otherwise the guards might feel the need to intervene and break things up. The comfort provided by these embraces was diminished somewhat by the strip searches the guards would conduct every time we would have visitors, patting us down both before and after we saw our loved ones.

As difficult as it may have been for my parents to come, I have to admit that the more I saw them, the more grateful I became that they were there. So much had changed in such a short period of time, and with each new shift that occurred, I increasingly felt like the grip I held on my sense of self was becoming weaker and weaker. Regularly seeing and interacting with my family members helped me retain an idea of who I was. Although, truth be told, even this impression was one that I failed to get a tight grasp on. The years leading up to my sentencing had been filled with chaos, confusion, and a lot of inebriation. When I finally became sober while in prison, there wasn't much I could look back on with any sense of conclusiveness or real understanding.

Regardless of how clouded my vision of myself and my life was, my family's visits were immensely helpful and kept me tethered to the ground in moments when I felt as though I had been unexpectedly and viciously catapulted through the air. The further I progressed into the period of my sentence, the more frequent these feelings of tumult became, and the more each of their visits did to boost my mood. However, over time, I did my best to achieve as much of a sense of stability as I could. A big part of this was maintaining and cultivating the relationships I had established with some of my fellow inmates. Initially, these connections were crafted out of a need to get by, but they evolved over time into genuine connections that helped ease some of the anxiety and difficulty that comes part and parcel with a life behind bars.

But, as the old saying goes, all good things must come to an end, and believe me when I say that the South Florida prison system did everything it could to ensure that everything good ended as quickly as possible. My acclimation to life within the specialized camp was just beginning to take something resembling a stable shape when, one day, a prison official called my name. I was informed that, for the third time in just about as many months, I would be relocating and making my home in another part of the detention center. Moving to this new building meant that I was effectively plucked out of the network of friends and allies I had spent so much time constructing so carefully. Additionally, it also meant that I was much closer to Michael, as we were now residents at the same address.

Before I reminisce any further about my time in the new building, it's worth explaining how things worked in the Dade Correctional Institute, especially as it pertained to the sleeping situation. Back in the South Florida Reception Center, the setup was much more traditional, more like what you'd expect when you think of prison and its cells. In Dade, however, things were a bit different. There, in the new camp, we were housed in a building that had been allocated for sleeping. If you'd like to imagine it in terms of a cell, think one huge, open place holding space. In this space, you'd find row upon row of bunk beds with space for 70 men in total to sleep. Effectively, it was the world's worst sleep-away camp cabin. Because of the layout of this cabin, we should distinguish between cellmates and bunkmates from this point forward. I had the former at the South Florida Reception Center, but after my move to the new building in Dade, each of the other men in the camp became my cellmate. As you may have been able to deduce, each bunkmate I had was the person who occupied the bed either above or below me. Now that the logistics have been cleared up, we can proceed with our journey down memory lane.

In the new building, I began building up a support network yet again. For better or worse, this new group of people was just as cosmopolitan, and just as unnerving, as the one that populated my previous place of residence. After the move, my days were filled with a bunch of new faces and presences, not all of whom I particularly got along with. There was Charlie, a jovial, older Black man. He loved to laugh and directed much of his mirth right at me. In the same age range, though a bit closer to middle age, there was Caucasian Sam. He and I were bunkmates for a while, and I can't say that the experience was pleasant, as Sam was prone to ingesting his own feces. Keeping with the theme of severe change, the person who succeeded Sam as my bunkmate (or "bunkie," as we referred to one another back then) was named Jenkins. He had a love for words and had a daily routine in which he would pick up a dictionary, leaf through it, and commit a brand new word to memory. It's worth mentioning that Jenkins was purported to have murdered someone, though I was never able to find an appropriate moment to press him on the subject.

Similar in ethnicity to the excrement-loving Sam, though with an entirely different taste in snacks, was George. He loved nothing more than having a little treat and would always have a bite on him. Next I met Henry, who was also White and also old. Henry, however, was confined to a wheelchair, and much of our bonding happened as I wheeled him around, something I would regularly do. The polar opposite to my "friend" Henry was Jud, a Black inmate who had aligned himself with one of the many gangs the prison housed. Jud was an angry man, and fights seemed to be one of his favorite pastimes. And, of course, there was Michael. Now living in closer proximity to each other, our friendship started to develop. Soon enough, however, I realized that he only really had one goal, which was to secure as many substances as he could to feed his addiction. Fortunately, Michael and I weren't lumped together for very long, and he made his way out of the camp soon enough.

Although Michael's absence was somewhat of a relief, largely because it made my own attempt at sobriety slightly easier to enact, the days of difficulty were far from over. In the time after his departure, my sentence began to drag by, and the nights became harder. Sleep crept further and further away from me, leaving my anxiety to grow more intense and invade the space in my mind where rest was supposed to be. Not long after Michael left, George attempted to take his own life. A few nights before this, as I recall, he'd had a nightmare. As he tossed and turned in his sleep, he would repeat the word "father" over and over again. A few of us woke up from this, with a few of this number staying up through the night to watch over him. Even all these years later, this moment sticks with me as being one of the more profound experiences I had behind bars.

Though I had no idea what George was dreaming about, or whether his interaction with his dad in his unconscious was good or bad, simply hearing that word made me miss my father. Moreover, when I think of this event now, I am overwhelmed with how strong the sense of humanity is that I connect to it. Back then, things were so chaotic that you sometimes forgot that you were surrounded by people who, just like you, had taken some steps down the wrong road. Regardless of what had led to our gathering there in that open-plan dormitory, we were all still human. In that moment, hearing George call out for his parent in the quiet of the night, I felt more connected than ever to those around me.

Sometimes, life in prison can seem downright unbearable, especially if your mind doesn't allow you to look toward the light and see a way out. I count myself lucky in that regard, as I was there for a short enough period of time that the end was visible from a relatively early point onward. However, there was a part of me that knew this vision alone wasn't enough, and that I would have to do what I could to ensure that it was realized, and that I wouldn't be stuck in that space for a moment longer than I had to be.

Despite the fact that I had intentionally constructed a network of people I could surround myself with, I still found myself treading a path that was somewhat different from the others. Admittedly, though rebellion wasn't my intention by any means, my determination to remain myself—and to remain *by* myself—lead to the perception that I was somehow refusing to acquiesce to the demands stipulated by the prison hierarchy. In retrospect, this assessment was accurate, though I never resisted actively enough for it to be that apparent to me. What I was, in fact, doing was simply undermining its working ever so slightly. I refused to attach or align myself with a specific group and did my best to avoid becoming a member of one of the prison's gangs, which were large in number and violent in action. Knowing what I did about the way the system worked, joining the ranks of a gang may well have been the quickest, easiest way to ensure my protection. However, doing so would also have made me a target the next time an intergroup rivalry developed, something that occurred with an almost predetermined regularity. The latter didn't seem to be a particularly attractive price, even if the immediate payoff was likely to make things a bit better. Subsequently, I stuck to my individualistic guns, filling my free time with the people I had met along the way. My social interactions were populated by the inmates I taught, shared space with, or who had otherwise come to be significant players in my life. I was by no means alone, and going to sleep at night without worrying whether I was the target of a plot avenging a fallen comrade made me sleep all the more soundly. Well, as soundly as one cloud sleep in the presence of 69 other men.

# The Challenge

If there's one thing about the experience of being imprisoned that should be patently clear to everyone by now, it's that absolutely nothing lasts in a life behind bars. Well, that may not be entirely true, as strife made itself our constant companions from the moment those hoses were turned our way. Nevertheless, when it comes to longevity in that world, you'd be better off not holding your breath, as it all comes tumbling down sooner or later. As cruel as your time inside can be, what makes the tip of the knife feel even sharper is the fact that so many of the challenges you face are brought upon you by others, although the reminder that your own actions put you there remains with you almost constantly.

Take the school I had come to love so dearly. My tenure as teacher hadn't lasted very long when the classroom was shut for the first time. A while later, after a tumultuous few weeks in which I felt more lost than I had imagined I would, we were allowed to resume our classes. Again, this lasted only a little while before the place was shuttered again. This place, its people, and the feeling of being grounded it provided me with was too valuable to lose, and I went in search of answers. Thankfully, I wasn't alone in my frustration and confusion, and others who had frequented the school also wanted an explanation. This inspired some confidence in our attempt, as I was sure that the strength that numbers afforded us elsewhere would be carried over to our dealing with bureaucracy, as well.

Alas, my bolstering conviction was soon turned into humiliating naïveté, as the powers-that-be refused to provide us with any reason for their decision. Needless to say, the closure of the school was a devastating blow, as I had once again lost something I loved, something that kept me anchored when all my mind wanted to do was run away from sensibility as fast as it could. My despair was followed by boredom, which the others who lost their place of learning also experienced. Although none of my students were housed with me, their investment in the process, as well as the progress they had been making was enough to make me suspect that this loss affected them deeply. In a place where temperaments already tend to run high, sitting alone without anything to distract you can prove to be deadly.

As much as I'd like to end this anecdote with a particularly rousing recounting of how we refused their refusal, stood our ground, and got what we wanted, I'm afraid the story ends here. In its place, other difficulties arose—this time in the bright light of the yard. The closing of the school was the catalyst for the authorities to begin closing other buildings and imposing lockdowns more regularly. Crucially, the majority of the areas that were shuttered were those in which recreational and other activities took place. In the absence of pastimes, violence began to brew. In response to inmates acting out, the wardens conducted raids on a more frequent basis, reminding us that their boots were still very much on our necks. Though they were going easy on the pressure now, they could stomp down at any moment, snapping whatever (and whomever) was in their way.

Predictably, the raids and crackdown didn't have the effect they had hoped for, and the violence continued to spread throughout the prison, escalating in intensity with each passing day. Eventually, things came to a head out in the yard, and one of the inmates was slain at the hands of another. Luckily, I wasn't in the yard when the murder occurred, but none of us were exempt from hearing the event unfold. Even though many of us hadn't borne witness to the killing, the sound of the med-evac's propellers resounded throughout the entire complex. In one of the most chilling juxtapositions I've ever seen, the cacophony of the helicopters arrival drowned out everything else, and the sight of a lethally injured body soundlessly being lifted up over the yard underscored just how small each of us was as we stood in the shadow of this systems and its components— human and otherwise.

From there, what had already been bad immediately became worse. The restrictions were tightened, with even more lockdowns being imposed, and random, invasive searches conducted with frighteningly high frequency. Still, the problems among the inmates remained, and soon the helicopters were coming every week, with each turn of its propellers signaling the beginning of another cycle, another bout of violence, and another probable death. It was hard to know for sure whether another person lost their life to the violence that was constantly escalating within the prison walls, but based on first-hand accounts, surviving a stabbing perpetrated with shanks made from materials specifically selected for their ability to inflict fatal levels of harm would be pretty damn difficult.

The cycle continued for weeks on end with the acquisition of any kind of stability far, far out of our reach. Things were constantly thrown into tumult, meaning that none of the relationships I had worked so hard to forge could be maintained. We were constantly in and out of lockdowns, subjected to raids, and each new stabbing steeped the collective temperament deeper and deeper into mistrust. Consequently, old alliances began to fall apart and new connections were all but impossible to make. Slowly but surely, each person I had tethered myself to (and whose presence had afforded me some measure of protection) moved further and further away from me, worsening my isolation with each departure.

I remember feelings of incredible frustration making themselves known during this chaotic period, though they were directed more at the outside world than anyone inside the prison itself. It wasn't lost on me for a moment that what was happening to us was being allowed by those in power. What also did not go unnoticed was the fact that I was serving my sentence in the 21st century, in the country that prides itself on being the best in the world. God knows Americans cling to that top spot with everything they have. And yet, here in the land of the free and the home of the brave, we were stripped of everything short of our skin.

They took away all we had, including our humanity. To my mind, this type of treatment (and of red-blooded Americans, no less) should have elicited public outcry for change and accountability. What I failed to account for was the fact that, in the eyes of the country, we were subhuman. We had committed crimes, and as such deserved every punitive measure that came our way, regardless of who we were or what had happened to make us break the law in the first place. It was clear that, in the US's quest for continuous development, it had left behind those members of its society who needed help the most. I could be outraged all I wanted, but no help was ever going to come.

To further drive this nihilistic point home, allow me to share with you the details of how things became even worse. You may be shocked to think that there's space beneath rock bottom, but believe me, however low you think people can sink, there are always some who can go lower. Case in point: The stranger who came up to me one day in the yard, when restrictions had been slightly relaxed, providing me with a false sense of hope that was erased nearly as quickly as it arose. Without any preamble to speak of, he informed me that it would be in my best interest to willingly surrender myself to one of the gangs operating in the prison. More specifically, he informed me that I had to give myself up for trade, which would allow the gang members to act as my pimps, essentially turning me into a bargaining chip or an object to be sold—or rented, rather, as there was no getting out of that position once you had given in. As you can imagine, his "advice" completely floored me, something I guess he read on my face; he went on to say that I should keep my reaction to a minimum. An outburst, he said, might lead to me being seen as confrontational and would certainly increase the risk of someone forcing themselves on me.

Not long after this interaction in the yard (which ended as suddenly and as quietly as it began), I became aware of the fact that I was being watched. Knowing what I know now, it's clear to me that there had been eyes on me for a while. However, I first became privy to this information when my locker was raided. While this was hardly a rare occurrence, it did have a rather devastating impact on me, as I had lost my possessions, the snacks my family had given me (which were as good as gourmet delicacies behind bars), and all the items that made up the jail's currency. The latter could be used to buy things from other inmates or as bargaining chips during negotiations. The theft occurred not long after the trade conversation in the yard, leading me to understand for the first time that I wasn't flying nearly as low under the radar as I had thought.

In the time that followed the raiding of my locker, things began to unravel further—and did so with alarming rapidity. By this point, Jenkins (the word-of-the-day learner) had become my bunkie, and his volatility was increasingly bubbling to the surface. However, before we get to Jenkins, we take a detour to Jud, whom you will remember as a perpetually irate gang member, and one of the people with whom I became acquainted after I was moved to the new building. Despite being somewhat familiar with each other, Jud and I were far from having any type of relationship. We knew each other in passing, nothing more, nothing less. In the end, however familiar we might—or might not—have been didn't matter, as Jud decided that I was the latest in a long series of people on whom he fixed his violent gaze.

As it transpired, he was the one who broke into my locker. More distressingly, Jud was also the one who had sent the messenger in the yard. However, the worst of the worst came one day when we were all coming in from yard, having just enjoyed the bit of fresh air that made its way beyond the prison walls. On this occasion, Jud announced to all who could hear that he had placed a bounty on my head. I didn't know where or when it was going to happen, or who my attacker would be, but I was assured that someone would be dispatched to rape and kill me. This, as Jud loudly proclaimed, was his intention, and he was dead set on seeing it through.

The death threats didn't stop there, and the second promise of violence sees us return to my cell—and to Jenkins. One day, not long after Jud had put a hit out on me, Jenkins came storming into the cell. To this day, I'm not sure who or what set him off, but all trace of the word-loving reader was gone entirely. In his place stood an enraged man whose presence in this cell with me was caused by the fact that he had already taken a life. Now, that same murderous fury shone through, the same fury that moved him to slap me clean across the face, an action he undertook without any provocation to speak of. Naturally, in his enraged state, I saw no reason why he couldn't use me as the scapegoat on which he pinned the blame for his aggression. I was the only thing standing before him, the only thing that (to him, at least) seemed weak enough for him to hurt, and he took his opportunity like a shot. No sooner had the slap begun echoing off the cell walls than Jenkins leaned in and, with a chilling sense of certainty, threatened to kill me in my sleep. In an incredibly short period of time, I had gone from an unremarkable face among the prison masses to the target of two separate, murderous intentions. All things considered, not the most tranquil few weeks I've had in my life. And with the solid proof of the last few weeks, I couldn't take any chances not believing these threats.

# The Solitary Outcome

In the first days of my time in prison, my only goal was to get by and to find a way to make 18 months (16 for good behavior, as it turned out) pass as quickly as I could. Never did I intend to make waves, achieve notoriety, climb the social ladder, or do anything that might potentially result in more attention being directed toward me. For the most part, this had to do with my interactions with the other inmates, and it was largely used as a survival mechanism. However, I wasn't very keen on drawing the eyes of the officers and other prison officials to me, either. As you can imagine, I was fairly successful in executing my plan—that is, until I became aware of the fact that my life was hanging much further out in the balance than I had imagined.

I won't cling to any pretense of bravado, trying to convince you that Jud's promise and Jenkins's threat was like water off a duck's back. I'm not sure that would work, to be perfectly honest, as I suppose nearly all of us would be terrified if they were delivered the promise of death on two separate occasions—while in prison. Before, the most effort my attempts at survival involved were just staying out of people's way and hoping they didn't notice me or think I had done them any wrong. Now, however, I had two people who perceived themselves to be slighted, who needed a scapegoat, and their ire had very much fixed a spotlight on me. My games of playing ostrich had completed their final round, and it was time for me to take action. Before you misconstrue my words as those indicating that an act of heroic bravery is about to occur, I hasten to remind you that I was still incarcerated in a place where, if the people you confronted didn't get to you, your beating would come at the hands of the guards. Violence and resistance were entirely out of the question. The only thing I could do was attempt to follow the system and hope that it would function properly, if only just this once.

My hope for help was pinned on a note that I planned on slipping into the officer's booth, appealing to the prison authorities for some sort of protection. As a sort of supplemental measure, I called my parents and let them know about my plan. From the very moment my message passed from my fingers, I felt the anxiety that had settled on my heart tightening its already vice-like grip. This was the only plan I had, and the only method short of physical combat I could think of that might ensure I live to see the outside world again. The very next day, an officer made his way from the observatory part of the dorm down to my bunk, handcuffs at the ready. The moment I saw him, I went numb from the shock. I had dared to let myself hope that help would arrive, but past experience had severely tempered my expectations. And yet there I was, hands bound behind my back being marched off to be taken into solitary confinement.

We arrive now at a critical juncture where I have to explain to you that, by handcuffing me and taking me to an isolated cell, the officer was saving my life. For a start, the arrest is standard procedure when someone is moved to solitary confinement. Admittedly, this is more so that the officers themselves are protected, as the prisoners are usually being moved because they have become violent with either the officers or their fellow inmates. Other infractions that resulted in a sentence to solitary confinement included disrespecting one of the officers, being in possession of items deemed to be contraband, and even walking too close to one of the female prison authorities. So, even though I was being transferred as a matter of security, the cuffs were part of the procedure. Moreover, in the Dade Correctional Institution, as in penitentiaries all over the US, solitary confinement served as more than just a punishment. Inmates who were regarded as being at risk of being targeted, assaulted, or otherwise accosted were also taken away from the general prison populace. This was done to ensure their safety, with the logic being that they could be protected more effectively if there was no one around them at all with the exception of the guards.

As an aside, I should mention that this was not my first brush with solitary confinement. Sometime before, I had come very close to doing some things that, if discovered, would have seen me cuffed and isolated in an instant. This was during those weeks when the revolving door of cellmates kept turning. Every so often, the old bunkie would leave and a new man would soon appear in his place (this was in the time before Jenkins's arrival). None of them were particularly appealing on any level, with many of them declaring their lewdness outright by masturbating in front of me. As disgusting as this harassment was, it did force me to confront the fact that I had been imprisoned for some time, and that my own sexual needs had gone unfulfilled for all that time. Though it hadn't exactly been a priority, having sexual acts shoved in my face (literally) drew my attention to just how touch-starved I had become.

As a result, I found myself being tempted to find someone with whom I could relieve the pressure. It was this temptation that meant I was dangerously flirting with the possibility of being sent to solitary confinement, as any inmates caught in compromising situations would be put in "the hole," as it was known. However, I was dissuaded from these pursuits by the prospect that any carnal engagement at all could see me end up in a transactional situation (which I was determined to avoid, as you know), lead to the establishing of a relationship, or otherwise lead to the contraction of an STI, something I had no desire to have.

When I was actually taken into solitary confinement, the experience was very much a mixed blessing. On the one hand, I was being escorted to a part of the prison where the murderous hands of Jenkins's or Jud's assassins couldn't reach me. On the other hand, however, my removal from my cell was done in plain view of about 70 other men, so it was by no means a subtle affair. To cap it off, Jenkins became enraged at the sight of me leaving and began screaming bloody murder. In between the expletives, he told me he knew that I had slipped a note to the officers.

With that one revelation, I had been branded a snitch. As far as social categories in prison go, that's just about the worst box you could be put in. This unpleasantness was compounded by some animosity on the part of the officer who was taking me into isolation. According to him, my father had called the prison a number of times, asking whether I had received protection yet, something I hadn't asked him to do. While his concern was touching, it worried me slightly, as it could have led to a whole other host of problems that would prevent me from accessing safety. However, regardless of these bumps along the way, I made it to my destination and was assured of at least one night without the threat of murder hanging over my head or sleeping in the bunk below mine.

# The Horrors

Although my newfound distance from those who had sought to harm me did provide me with a degree of solace, it wasn't lost on me that I had simply moved from one corner of this struggling world to another. Moreover, while the immediate threat on my life had been removed, it was clear as day that I was by no means out of the woods yet. In solitary confinement, whatever grip the authorities had on us was tightened to the point where becoming crushed under the weight of their thumb seemed to be an inevitability. And, distressingly, being taken to a place of safety similarly meant undergoing the stripping process again, albeit one that allowed you to maintain some more dignity than before.

Instead of asking us to take off our clothes, the prison officers instead relieved us of just about anything that might keep us tethered to our sanity. The only things I was allowed was some paper, a pen, and a few stamps that enabled me to stay in touch with my family. I clung to this lifeline, small as it was, with all my might, largely because it was the only way I could still be assured of the fact that life still existed beyond the ever-decreasing confines of the prison building.

Apart from this one sliver of light, my time in solitary was a period of immense darkness. The term "living nightmare" was, I believe, coined for the sole purpose of describing circumstances such as these. Never before had I wished for my senses to become weakened, but the sensory assault that greeted me day after day in the solitary confinement bloc meant that my mind had no choice but to follow such trains of thought. The smell of human excretions always lingered in the air, with urine and feces being the odors that predominately latched themselves onto the inside of my nostrils. Of course, such pungency never limits it manifestation to the world of the senses, and the smell of sewage drew legions and legions of cockroaches.

Believe me when I say that no amount of descriptive words, no matter how hyperbolic they may become, could ever paint an accurate picture of the number of bugs that were crawling inside those cells. The roaches were everywhere, crawling over everything they could, and flying into and over what they couldn't. Of all the experiences in solitary confinement, I still feel ill at ease thinking back to those insects. For as long as I can remember, I have been terrified of palmetto bugs, which are a particular type of cockroach, specifically the type that grows to be very large and can fly around. Though palmetto bugs weren't the only variety of roach to be found in the cells, they certainly constituted a not ungenerous portion of the insect population. The disgust elicited by the presence of these creatures truly cannot be understated. Every morning, after fighting to fall asleep the night before, waves of the bugs would come pouring out from underneath my mattress as soon as I started to stir and stretch.

In addition to living alongside these filthy exoskeleton-bearing creatures, solitary confinement did the best it could to remind all of us that we were, in fact, confined to the spaces that the guards and warden had decided on. When living among the general population, time spent in the yard would be allowed regularly, and time in the sun would often stretch over a couple hours. Though this was by no means enough to make up for the dark damp of the prison interior, it contributed to relieving a bit of tension. In solitary, however, we were only allowed to see the outside for about an hour a day. But even this small indulgence was anything but reliable. As time went on and the conditions inside the prison became worse, with riots and violence becoming regular occurrences, lockdowns were imposed all the more frequently. Of course, when the entire building is kept under lock and key, allowing us to see some direct light fell further and further down the guards' list of priorities. With that being said, there were some things you could depend on in solitary. The first is definitely having near-constant encounters with insects, with the second being the clockwork-like delivery of food, which was achieved by sliding a tray with food underneath the door of the cell. I feel compelled to mention that, in this instance, the word "food" is used very, very loosely.

Time dragged on in solitary confinement, with the days and night becoming blurred together. I'm not sure how long I was there before the first visitor came, but it may as well have been years, for all I was able to tell. The first person who came to see me was a prison sergeant, whose presence in front of my cell was investigation-motivated. Admittedly, this makes our meeting sound much more spy-like than it actually was, as he was only there to ask me (through a crack in the cell door) about the events that had led to my removal from the general population. Regardless of the ambience of our encounter, the sergeant's trip was made in vain. Though he pressed me on the matter, I refused to divulge the name of the person who had placed the bounty on my head. Though I didn't care much for Jenkins or Jud on a personal level, I had been in prison for long enough to understand what sharing this information might mean for me. There was no such thing as a secret in that world, and I had already been labelled a snitch when I'd first been arrested and brought to solitary. Though I by no means deserved the moniker (at least not to my mind), there was no way I was going to run the risk of making it a legitimate designation. Despite my reticence, the sergeant assured me that he would find the person he was looking for, and that he would ensure the appropriate punishment was handed down.

Not long after this meeting, the second visitor arrived at the door of my cell. This time, however, it was a familiar face that came calling. I had worked with the chaplain during my time as the prison teacher, and we had established a relationship that was as close to friendship as two people in our positions could come. We'd gotten along well, and she was a source of great (but stern) support during the chaotic period of school closures and reshuffles. Now, standing just outside a moldy, roach-filled cell, the nature of our connection remained unchanged. The reason for her visiting me was very different from that of the sergeant and his fact-finding mission. The chaplain had come to see me, to visit with me, and to find out how I was doing. I'm not sure how much she knew about what life in isolation was like and whether she was motivated to come see me because she knew the truth of my circumstances. Whatever the reason, I'm glad she found her way to my cell that day. I hadn't seen anyone who was close to my heart for a while at that point, and seeing a friendly face made me feel exponentially more human than I had felt in a long time. Although my family had kept up a steady stream of postal communication, even after I was put into confinement, having a mostly friendly physical presence before me was more bolstering than I could have imagined. Also, it made me miss my loved ones even more, but I understood that it had to do for the time being.

The happiness brought on by the chaplain's visit was doomed to be short-lived when, out of nowhere, a guard showed up in front of the cell door, depositing my new cellmate inside. If this shocks you, you can imagine how I felt in that moment. As I would eventually learn, there were some instances in which solitary confinement tended to be light on the whole isolation thing. Specifically, these instances arose when two of the prisoners' move away from the general population had been conducted for protection purposes. Allocating more than one inmate to a cell in solitary confinement was also a matter of space, as there simply weren't enough cells for all of us to be completely isolated. Only those who had proved to be very violent could be assured of complete and total isolation.

As it transpired, both Joe (my new cellmate) and I had been under some sort of threat, and as such had been thrown together as a matter of convenience. The reasoning behind our being placed in the same cell stemmed from the fact that, in the situations that had led to our solitary confinement, neither one of us had been the perpetrator. Consequently, I imagine they assumed that neither one of us was a threat to anyone else. Well, you know what they say about assumptions.

Joe hadn't been there five minutes before he started sizing me up. Though this, in and of itself, is relatively innocuous, my past experiences made me more than wary of this new person I would be sharing a living space with. In the end, my intuition would prove to be correct. Not long after he arrived, Joe made the first of several offensive, violent moves. He started by calling me over to the window fitted into the cell door, ostensibly under the guise of spotting something interesting. From that point onward, things went downhill fast. While I was trying to find what I was told to look out at, Joe stood behind me with his penis in his hand, making attempts to rub it against me. Whatever discomfort I already felt around him was multiplied a hundred times over, and I did my best to move from him as quickly as I could. This was the wrong move to make.

Joe became enraged and began searching for a weapon with which to punish me for rebuking his advances. In the absence of anything obviously harmful, he stuffed a bar of soap inside one of his socks and proceeded to beat me. In between blows, I pleaded with Joe to stop. I told him over and over again that I had no interest in sex in general, at least not while I was in prison. As he continued, I explained that I was in our cell for protection and for nothing else. After a while, it seemed as though some of my words got through to him, and the assault abated. In time, Joe calmed down and bizarrely decided that this was the perfect moment to strike up a conversation with me. The strangeness of the decision wasn't lost on me, but I went with it for fear of undergoing another round of soap-based assault. Throughout the course of our conversation, I learned a great deal about Joe. More specifically, I learned that the reason he had been imprisoned in the first place was the committing of several murders. His move to solitary confinement, however, was brought about by an attempt on his life. Another inmate had tried to kill Joe with a shank, hence his presence in our cell and the large scar than ran across his face.

That interaction saw the start of an uneasy truce between me and Joe. I can't say that we ever became friendly, something I attribute in large part to the fact that his first few days in our cell were characterized by him sexually assaulting me, as well as the physical altercation that followed. Nevertheless, things didn't get as bad as that for the rest of the time we spent as cellmates. I'm not really sure how long he and I were in there together. What I do know is that it came to an end relatively quickly. One day, a guard showed up, handcuffed Joe, and took him away. To this day, I have no idea where he went, nor have I seen him since. I can't admit that I was particularly upset by his departure, as his presence always made me uneasy, and there was a part not entirely in the back of my head that was on constant, high alert for the repetition of any past offenses on his part. True to fashion, Joe made it relatively easy for me to be okay with him being gone, as he lifted some of my letters and stamps, taking them with him when he left. I only realized this after my cell became mine again, and did wonders to dispel any feelings of abandonment and curiosity I might have had.

My feelings of relief after Joe was taken away were soon replaced with feelings of fear and anxious anticipation. They manifested a while after Joe had gone, when the cell opposite mine had a new occupant. I remember seeing guards bring him in through the tiny window in my door. I recognized him immediately, before I had even seen his face clearly. Somehow, Jud had found his way back to me. His appearance sent shivers down my spine and filled both my days and nights with more fear than I had felt since Joe's arrival. The person who had placed a bounty on my head and threatened me with certain death had now taken up residency across the hall from me in the safest place there was in this prison.

I was immediately filled with fear and began to wonder when (and how) Jud's retaliation would come. Oddly enough, it didn't. Though I was sure he would start screaming and cursing again at the first sight of me, all he did was wave once he noticed I was his new neighbor. To make matters even more confusing, his wave appeared to be friendly and completely devoid of malice. His nonchalance at seeing his once-intended victim so close to him floored me. I had no idea why he was there, and why he hadn't come for me as soon as he could. I knew that there was no way he could actually reach me, given our physical separation by the cells. And yet somehow, the fear I had that he would find his way to me was oddly alleviated by his single, friendly wave.

Given the history between us and the events that had led to our separation, this sudden and significant shift in Jud's demeanor baffled me. All I could think was that the sergeant had managed to find the information he was looking for, and that he had indeed followed through on his punitive promise. Regardless of how shocked I was, Jud was there and so was I, along with my nervous anticipation. Days went on, and my being on edge increasingly seemed to be for nothing. Jud made no motion in my direction. In fact, he didn't even attempt to. It was as if the slate was wiped clean. Then, morning broke one day, and the hustle and bustle of the hallway seemed to be more intense than usual.

I can't tell what's going on, but something has happened. The noise surges and several screams follow one another. Moments later, they shut off the water. Then, the lights go and I am plunged into darkness. The rest of the hallway is, as well, and the chaos grows and grows, crescendoing right before the lights come back on. When they do, a figure hovers in the distance. I walk to window and see that it's floating in the cell opposite me. Soon, the figure comes into focus, and I can see that it is Jud. He has hanged himself in his cell.

My heart feels as though it's falling through my stomach from the shock, but there is no time to deal with my surprise. The noises and banging sounds are growing in intensity. The louder they become, the harder the people around me start screaming until a never-ending cacophony of shouts resound throughout the building. It feels to me as though the very walls of the prison are shaking—which I believe is caused by a number of other inmates banging against the walls and stomping on the floors as hard as they can, using whatever is at hand to contribute to the din. The screams go on for a long time, and then they stop. It's as though someone has cut straight through each screamers' vocal cords, and a harsh silence falls on the unit. In the absence of noise, my mind begins to turn, and a million thoughts start to race through my consciousness. Only one makes it through the melee, and it's the clearest thought I've had in a while: Whatever happens in the future, I can never come back to a place like this. As I make this conviction, I feel the despondence start to set in. Tears start to fall, and it's as though they are washing away all my strength. I slide down to the floor, where I remain, weeping.

At one point, the flow of tears dislodges something in my mind. It's that quote from the Bible that my father would sometimes repeat when I was younger, and that still sticks with me even well into adulthood. My father repeated this quote once more in one of the letters he wrote to me during my period of incarceration. Perhaps that's why its floating so close to the surface of my consciousness at the moment when I need it the most. My affiliation with the word of God had ended several years prior, but now seemed as good a time as any to have a come-to-Jesus moment. And while the sound of my father's voice didn't exactly make me yearn for a return to His flock, it did get me through those last difficult days.

In case you don't recall, that verse states the following: "No temptation has overtaken you except what is common to mankind. And God is faithful; he will not let you be tempted beyond what you can bear. But when you are tempted, he will also provide a way out so that you can endure it." As these words run through my mind with my body contorted into a fetal position on the floor, tears still streaming down my face, something falls into place somewhere in my heart. Somehow, I know there will be a way out of this darkness. But in order to find my escape, I have to endure the shadows for a while longer.

Chapter 7:

# Hitting the Reset Button

Sixteen months of my life were spent behind bars. As much as I understood that my imprisonment was the result of my recklessness and the addiction that gave rise to it, it must be said that any time spent in jail or prison is unpleasant, to say the least. It makes sense, all thing considered, and I would often hear officers reminding inmates that where we were was not, after all, a Holiday Inn.

Every day that passed, the authorities would make sure we understood the reality of the place in which we found ourselves. That being said, for all the horrors I saw and lived, the experience was nothing short of transformative. The next part of my story picks up some time before I was allowed to live my life outside of the confines of a cell or exercise. Soon after my release, perhaps even before, I knew that things could never go back to the way they were. I wasn't exactly sure how it would happen, or if I could do it at all, but I was determined to hit the reset button, start from scratch, and finally get to building the life that had eluded me for so many years.

## A Conviction Is Made

Spending time within the American prison system is sobering in more ways than I could ever begin to comprehend. In the nearly year-and-a-half I spent as an inmate, the number of experiences I had that permanently changed me could fill the pages of a book, albeit one I would never be able to revisit after writing. The horrors of my time in solitary confinement are memories I still find my mind wandering back to from time to time, albeit involuntarily. However, I do count myself lucky that my time in prison didn't end in that lonely cell. Had I walked from there back out into the real world, I'm not sure that my mind (or, in fact, my heart) would have been able to withstand the shock of such a tremendous, sudden change.

Thankfully, the time leading up my release was one of transition and reacclimating. I was released back into the general population not long after Jud's probable passing. I can't be certain about his fate, as there was no way to know whether the guards made it to his cell before he died. Moreover, the sight of his body hanging in the air was more than I could stomach, and it wasn't long before I had to turn away. Though I have to admit that the entire ordeal still stuck with me, my release from solitary meant that it was time to move on, something I was all too glad of.

My return to the general population was a relief, and although it was far from the happiest place I'd ever been, simply being around other people made me feel more joy than I had in weeks, if not months. My release from solitary confinement had, in reality, a bit more change to it than simply being out and about among the other inmates. Upon leaving that single-person cell, I was put on a bus and shipped back to the building at the South Florida Reception Center where I had first made my entry into this twisted world. There, I was allowed back into the yard once more, although not on an entirely regular, daily basis. Still, the mere fact that I could stand out in the sun, free from the weight of death threats and bounties made me appreciative of whatever time I could spend outside, however irregular its occurrence may be.

Coming back from solitary confinement, things were much different from what they had been before. This struck me as odd. Nothing in the prison had changed, and the system still treated us as miserably as ever. So, in the absence of any noticeable alterations, I had to assume that the change had taken place somewhere inside me. This time, when I was around other people, our interactions were more pleasant. Lighter, even. I rediscovered my ability to entertain and managed to make those around me laugh in a way that I hadn't been able to—or inclined to, if I'm honest—when I started this whole freedomless journey. This laughter stood out to me for a number of reasons, not only because I was the one who managed to elicit it.

These laughs were the first ones I had heard in a long time that weren't tinged with ulterior motives or undertones of evil. Moreover, it was the first time in a long time that I was able to join in with the fun. As affirming as this experience was, its arrival did come with a pang of yearning, as I was reminded how much I loved performing, and how much I missed the stage. I feel compelled to mention that my time in prison did not pass without at least a bit of showbiz razzle-dazzle, as I had assumed the role of a bombastic preacher in a play. Notably, my most memorable contribution to the production was urging my fellow inmates to repent their sins, lest they burn in the fires of hell. Of course, because I enjoyed making others laugh, the prison authorities couldn't allow it to go on for too long, and I was reprimanded by the officers in charge. Thankfully, an apology was enough to get me off the hook. As annoyed as I wanted to be by the fact that such an innocent thing had been deemed cause for concern, I was reminded that I had to tread very carefully. The end of my sentence was fast approaching, and there was no way I would jeopardize my chance at freedom.

I recall an experience I had earlier on in my sentence that helped to cement my intention to do what it took to see the end of my prison days as soon as possible. One day, in a break between teaching sessions, the chaplain and one of the inmates got to talking, and their conversation soon turned into a discussion on recidivism. As the two of them spoke, the chaplain said, "The only ones who come back to prison are the ones who don't make it a conviction to never return." The moment I heard those words, it was as if every light in every room in my mind was suddenly turned back on.

You see, I'm well aware of what convictions are. I know that to be convicted means to be determined (in one sense of the word). More specifically, conviction means possessing a determination so strong that nothing, neither good things nor bad, can get in the way of you reaching your goal. Conviction is following through at all costs. It's what moves a person beyond contemplation and preparation, and into a place of action. It isn't something you have to announce or explain to others. The only person who has to be convinced of your determination is yourself, and so I made it a conviction that I would never return here again, not once those gates had been opened for me. This recollection peeked out from the recesses of my mind when I was in solitary confinement, and I can still remember making that promise to myself with tears streaming down my face.

In the time after that reprimanding, I was reminded several times of the fact that I wasn't destined to be a permanent citizen of the world behind bars. Not only was this something I repeated to myself time and time again, but it was also echoed by the officers with whom I spoke on several occasions. From both sources, the sentiment was clear: Keep your eyes on the prize; your time here is almost over. For a few weeks, thoughts of the end of my sentence kept mulling around my head.

Then, one day the news finally came, and I was informed by the prison authorities that the end of my sentence was imminent, and that I would be released when my 16 months came to an end. As amazing as this news was, I have to confess that it did nothing for my nerves. Now, with each day that my release crept closer, I became more and more anxious. In particular, my anxiety revolved around being the recipient of more threats, bodily harm, or intimidation. Freedom was so close that I could taste it, and so I made sure to do my best to stay away from anything that might even vaguely resemble trouble. My efforts seemed to work, and I made it to only a few days before I was set to go before a hurdle was thrown across my path.

Part of the release process of the American prison system involves taking a few identifying photographs before an inmate is released back into the world. One of the criterion for taking these photos includes being clean-shaven. When my turn in front of the camera came, I prepared by shaving the night before. By the time I was stood in front of the lens, however, some stubble had grown in. It was enough to be noticed, but not nearly enough to be considered anything close to a legitimate beard.

Unfortunately, this was not a sentiment that the officer in charge of the process shared. Upon seeing my slightly-less-than-clean-shaven face, she flew into a rage and threatened to report me to the prison authorities for lying and disobedience. The officer refused to take any photos until I marched myself back to my cell and shaved again. Although I acquiesced and made the trip, my heart was going wild inside my chest. At first, upon hearing her threat, it dropped straight to the bottom of my stomach.

However, once a few moments had passed and I was on my way back to the razor, my pulse shot up in anger. In an instant, I became incredibly frustrated with myself. I couldn't believe that I had let my chance at freedom come so close to slipping through my fingers—and over such a trivial thing, too. My anger was only intensified by the realization that, had I actually gotten a citation from the officer, I would be remanded back into custody and face further jail time. Had this happened, the two-months-early release for good behavior I had managed to get would have gone straight down the drain. I was furious with myself, possibly more than the situation warranted, but my nerves were fried to begin with.

After this, the last day of my incarceration couldn't come fast enough. Even though I knew that the time would pass in the same way that it always had, I became like a little child waiting for Christmas morning so they could open their presents. I suppose in my case, it was more like the day before my parents' anniversary, when we would all be eagerly waiting to open our gifts. Regardless, what little patience I had was rapidly fizzling away, and though I wanted desperately to do something with my anticipatory energy, I found myself immobilized out of fear that any action at all might cost me the freedom that I could feel brushing along my fingertips. So, frustrated as I was, all I could do was bide my time and wait for the day to come. At last, thank God, it did.

The morning of my release, an officer knocked on the bars of my cell, telling me to pack my things. Once I had collected my meager possessions, I was taken to another new holding cell, where I was kept for hours before being visited by the prison warden. In my head, the time spent in his office would drag on for ages, during which I would have to jump through all sorts of hoops to show that I was worthy of being released. As is often the case, my mind ran away from itself, making me anxious about events that would never transpire. As it happened, all the warden did was look over my release papers before uttering two simple sentences in my direction: "Looks like you need to lay off the juice, man. Good luck." His well-wishes marked the end of our meeting, as well as the end of my time in prison.

From his office, I was taken out of the jail and into the arms of my anxiously awaiting parents.

Our meeting was every bit as emotional as you can imagine, although the expression of these emotions was largely limited to my mother. She hugged me tightly, crying as she did so. While embracing her, I felt that I should also shed a few tears, if only because of the momentousness of the occasion. But I couldn't do it. In the months leading up to our reunion, I had seen, heard, and spilled enough tears of my own that the well inside me had run dry. Though I knew was happy to be back with them, there was barely any feeling in my heart at all. Too much had happened. And although I understood that my time behind bars was the result of my own doing, I knew that there were many, many things that had contributed to that part of my life. I had to leave all those things behind now and find a way to become better than I had been before. My nightmare had ended, and I was now fully awake at the start of a new chapter. I had no idea what the future would bring, but I knew my work had only just begun.

# A Change Is Determined

In the age of invention, innovation, and improvement, it's likely that so many of us have come to believe that change is instantaneous, regardless of what's actually being modified. While this swiftness would certainly be nice, and would undoubtedly make so many of life's processes much, much easier, real change takes a lot more time. Also, it takes a hell of a lot more effort. My most extensive experience with change, up to this point in time, had been with Alcoholics Anonymous' (AA) 12-step program. The irony is not lost on me that, by telling you about it now, the acronym's second "A" loses some of its punch. More importantly, this was also one of my more educational experiences with change. I feel it necessary to point out that my presence at meetings wasn't entirely my own choice. Because of my past offenses and my DUI (well, DUIs in plural, I suppose), this program became a mandatory component of my recovery, both in terms of my addiction and my standing as a contributing member of society. Completing each of those 12 steps successfully meant confronting my past in its entirety—without skipping over or ignoring any of the parts that I would rather forget.

Essentially, I was forced to take a look at how things had been and at what I had done in those years when the majority of my waking hours were lived under the influence. The AA program, painful as it was at times, taught me so much more than I had expected. Through honest engagement with the past, I came to see that change is messy and unpleasant. Change is also nonlinear, and it's more than likely that whatever order you expected things to proceed in will be far, far removed from reality. Moreover, change is very rarely seen through on the very first try. This doesn't mean that you should give up, or even that you put your efforts on hold. Rather, reckoning with this means understanding that moving on from something as deeply influential as substance addiction is extremely difficult. This difficulty comes in part from the fact that, despite the guidance of the steps, you really don't have any idea what you're doing. Consequently, setbacks become part of the process. Though I learned this in the context of recovering from drug and alcohol addiction, I'm pretty sure the principles of change remain more or less the same across the board.

In my case, the combined processes of change and recovery meant gaining more and more understanding the further along I went. For the most part, this understanding had to do with my determination to never set foot in a prison again as long as I lived—or at least to never set foot in a prison as an inmate ever again. My success with this resolution was, I discovered, predicated on first achieving a number of subgoals, each of which required just as much conviction on my part. Looking back on it now, it's slightly surprising just how comprehensive these goals were, stretching over nearly every aspect of my life. The effect that prison had on me was incredibly profound, and much of it still sticks with me to this day.

As such, I suppose I shouldn't have been that shocked to find that past version of me set his sights on amending and ameliorating as many things as possible. The surprising goals in question were more than two years in the making and included stopping the use of substances altogether, figuring out how I could fall in love with myself and the person I was, as well as finding a way to deal with my past and put it to rest. The idea was that this would allow me to bring my awareness to the present fully, and to improve myself and the future I hoped to achieve.

As I'm sure you can imagine, reaching each of these aims wasn't easy, especially after years of self-abuse, self-hate, and the cultivation of less-than-healthy habits. Nevertheless, my determination never wavered. I'd like to pretend that this also means that things were smooth sailing from the outset, but the truth was something much different. In the two years that it took me to achieve those subgoals, I was also fighting to hold on to the sobriety I had managed to establish while still behind bars.However, I found myself slipping back into old habits on more than one occasion, albeit less severely than I had in the past. In the moment, these slips and lapses were discouraging, and I can't pretend that there weren't moments of frustration. However, by the time I was taking my sobriety seriously, I had learned a lot. Among the many things I had come to realize was the fact that I had spent the better part of a decade cycling through one set of harmful and dangerous behaviors after the other. I knew not to expect massive, fundamental, lasting change overnight, but I still found my morale dragged down every time a drink or a drug would inch its way back into my life. So while I can't pretend that those experiences were enjoyable, their effect on me was significantly weaker than it would have been even a year before.

# A Renegotiation of Relationships

Now, before we stray too far into life coach territory, let's talk some more about change—specifically, the changes I was encouraged to make during my time in

AA. Chief among them was a change distilled into three key components: people, places, and things. Making changes focusing on these three things is a mainstay of the program it aims to shift those in recovery away from situations, locales, persons, and even objects that may prove triggering, and which may potentially send them careening back down that spiral of abuse and addiction. However, while the idea of removing these things from your life is a good idea in theory, the actual execution is much more difficult and much more nuanced. Although meetings take place in a group setting, the program encourages you to change these things almost in isolation. Group sessions are perhaps what people think of first when AA comes to mind, but in truth, the hard work really happens outside these meetings.

Essentially, you can just switch up some of the places you frequent or change up some of the things you use in your everyday life. Additionally, you can also just make some alterations to the people in your life. In real life, however, things aren't that simple. In some instances, these people or places cannot be changed, and you have to take another tack. When this happens, its the relationship itself that has to change, with the person in recovery having to overhaul the boundaries that exist within and around the connection, as well as remolding some of the smaller, more nuanced aspects of the relationship, whatever its nature may be.

Given how complicated the years preceding my entry into recovery were, it makes sense that the changes I tried to implement required more effort than the AA program's theory purported. While I would certainly have liked to simply hear "people, places, and things" and jump into action, fixing and improving these left and right, it turns out that I had to take the longer, more extensive road to healing. Things weren't simple enough for me to perform a quick reshuffle. Instead, the onus fell upon me to re-evaluate everything in my life, relationships included, and determine what could be worked on and what needed to come to an end. Before this could happen, however, there were other preparatory steps I had to take as part of my recovery. Included among these was the making of amends with those who had been impacted by my drug and alcohol abuse. The name given to the practice is deceptively simple, and the act itself requires a lot more sincerity, as well as making a commitment to change. When making amends as part of the twelve-step program, you not only apologize for your misdeeds, but you do what is required or asked of you in order to begin healing the wounds you inflicted upon the hearts and minds of others. In addition to this, I was tasked with a renegotiation focusing on each connection I had in this world. During this process, not only was the health of the relationship assessed but also its viability moving forward.

When it came to my friends, this meant putting all my cards on the table, not only about my addiction, but also about my recovery and the hopes I had for how it would progress. Though I'm wary of stating that an ultimatum was made, the term will suffice in the absence of another. The first option of said ultimatum presented to my friends was the continuation of the relationship, but this time with the understanding that the past would be left there. In the present and moving forward, there would be no drugs, there would be no alcohol, and there would no more drama. Instead, our friendships would be built on respect for and comprehension of the fact that I was making new, better decisions, ones that would see me move away from the life I lived before, and away from the person I had been. Alternatively, should they not be able to accept this, our time in one another's lives would come to an end. Not to spoil things for you too quickly, but there weren't very many people who decided that the first option was something they were interested in.

Things were slightly different when it came to the "people, places, things" process with my family. Where my other relationships were provided with an "or," it seemed clear to me that only one option could be presented in this context. Though I never actually offered any of my family an ultimatum, I think it was clear to all of us that refusal to accept the changes I was making, and the growth I was experiencing, would lead us down another, more estranged path. Fortunately, that alternative has never been explored.

What happened instead was the reaching of a point of understanding between myself, my parents, and other members of my extended family. I implemented changes in these relationships as well. For my family, however, they were much closer to absolute statements than anything else. I had hidden and contorted my identity around their perceptions, beliefs, and values for too long. I had made enough mistakes to understand that there was no time like the present to start living as yourself. This was more or less what I told them, albeit with slightly more emotional undertones. That particular conversation was more about making them understand—more specifically, getting them so far as to comprehend that my continued health and sobriety depended on getting closer to the things that were important to me. This included, in no small part, having the ability to openly and freely love whomever I want, and not be forced to believe that those feelings (which had always been a natural energy emitted from my heart) were undesirable, evil, or subhuman.

To be honest with you, while this conversation was certainly a statement to them, it was also a powerful moment of reclamation for me. No longer would I simply lie down or roll over when presented with arguments that sought to demonize my identity or reduce my feelings and the love I held in my heart to abnormalities or symptoms of spiritual illness. Letting go of these notions and submissive or repressive behaviors also meant finally letting go of the things that had led to my sickness and strife in the first place. My perception of this release occupies a strange place in my mind, if only because I also understand that the illnesses I suffered served a larger purpose. To me, these negations of who I am and the rejection of what I felt acted like a poison that sent shooting pains through my heart, soul, and mind. To others, however, upholding these beliefs was a means of gaining and maintaining security. In doing so, they felt they had more control of the world around them and found a way to flourish. It's regrettable that two such polar opposites can exist, especially within the context of one human life, but the division of the lived experience into such extreme binaries is one of the key coping strategies society employs.

Regardless of the truth of past situations, I feel compelled to mention that the assignation of blame is by no means the goal with all of us. I don't fault my parents for their beliefs, or even for their promotion of views, values, and actions that so clearly and severely oppose my existence. It's what they need to thrive and to make sense of the larger world around them. Still, if I was ever to achieve something resembling a healthy recovery, it was important for them to understand that the very ambrosia that sustained their souls acted much more insidiously when exposed to my spirit. And for the most part, that understanding took place. While I can't say that our relationship is perfect, most days my parents and I manage to exist within a happy medium that works as a win-win (mostly). As time has passed, all of us have realized that we're stuck being the way we are, for better or worse. Though our identities and perspectives do sometimes clash, what brings us back to that middle way is remembering that none of us can change the other. Acceptance will always be part of the journey, and ironically, we just have to make our peace with that.

Just to give you an idea of how far-ranging this renegotiation and re-evaluation was, the relationships I examined included not only those I had with my parents, the rest of my family, and my friends, but also the link between myself and God. Somehow, the latter had never become entirely severed, and while I can't say that the answer I've settled on regarding my connection to a higher power is the one I expected, it's certainly better than the position I previously held. My reconciliation with the divine has largely been based on the idea that some sort of creator does indeed exist somewhere in the cosmos, at least from my perspective. I have to admit that getting to a place where I can admit this wasn't easy, and I spent a lot of time agonizing over whether I actually believed in any sort of higher power in the first place, especially one that would allow so many injustices and so much suffering to pass. Part of what convinced me, I suppose, is the fact that whatever higher entity exists out there does allow good things to arise along with the bad. Truth be told, these good things can sometimes become easily overshadowed by their negative counterparts. For me, what it all comes down to is that nature and humanity are both entirely too complex, intelligent, and beautiful not to have come from some sort of creator.

My final judgment came when I discovered that I could re-evaluate God in the same way I had done with the others. In doing so, I could essentially reinvent Him and gain a new understanding of what he's all about. Eventually, this new comprehension took place, and I decided that God does exist, just not in the way I was taught.

Instead, he exists in the form of pure, unconditional love, the same love showed to me by my parents during those long months filled with cancer treatments; the same love given to me by my parents during my darkest hours. It dawned on me that I could find God in my mother and father, in myself, in nature, in the world at large, and in the love my parents had always shown me, and which they continue to afford me.

# Learning to Love Oneself

Achieving sobriety was hands-down one of the hardest things I have ever done in my life. A close second would be undertaking the process of learning to love myself. Once I found myself breathing the pure air, free from prison walls, I decided that it was time to determine who I had become. Moreover, it was time to start loving that person, something I'd never even thought of attempting before. In the past, any and all forms of self-love had only been developed from those identities I had crafted or assumed out of a need to survive and fly under the radar. As a result, the space my real self was supposed to take up remained empty. Whenever someone would say something kind to the person I was pretending to be, that vacuum grew deeper and darker. Every form of validation I received felt hollow, largely because the person to whom it was expressed didn't exist. What did exist was the mask I put on to become this person that people complimented, accepted, or otherwise liked.

This pattern of pretending carried on for decades, beginning in early childhood and establishing itself as part of my functioning by the time I was in middle school. Now, in adulthood, as I embarked on a journey of self-improvement, I found that I was lost. I knew that I wanted to get better and improve myself, but I had absolutely no idea what that betterment might look like. Try as I might, I could not formulate any picture of my personhood in my head. All that was there was that emptiness from before. That space meant that no part of my journey could continue before I determined who the person walking this road actually was. For the first time in my life, I had to look inward and decide which aspects of what I found there were real and authentic to me, and which had been affected or assumed. Moreover, I had to determine what my values were, and which parts of the identity I possessed aligned with them. In a nutshell, I had to decide what and who I would be from that moment onward. To be perfectly honest with you, though the results changed my life, I hated this particular process.

How long had I walked the Earth without anything resembling a concrete sense of self? How long did I have to create something that might make me feel even just slightly like myself? Instead, I had jumped from one contextual character to another, hoping that no one would see through the façade. Although it had proven to be successful in the moment, I was now left with nothing I could claim as my own, and I hated that. I hated what I had allowed myself to become. I hated how others had made me feel in the past, and despised even more the fact that I had allowed their words to affect me so deeply, so much so that I believed every single thing they said about me.

At some point, realization began to shine through the thick clouds of hatred and regret. Whatever I had been in the past, while wrong on many levels, wouldn't serve me moving forward. Because I had no use for that old version of myself, it was best to leave him in the past. In his place I would build the person that would reach the finish line of this marathon of change, although I'd probably have to go through many more 5Ks after that for the rest of my life. This person was the only who could walk the road that lay ahead of me, the only one who would someday allow me to reach a place where I could look at who I was and love what I saw. I've been that person for a while now, and I've stopped more than once to look at who I have become. While it's nowhere near as bad as it once was, I must confess that I still struggle with the whole concept of "loving yourself." At least as it pertains to me loving myself.

There are moments when voices from the past will pipe up again, and it's in those moments that my capacity for this type of love becomes especially shaky. And yet, as the years roll by, those same voices can't reach the same volume they once could. By now, the noise comes only as a whisper. Granted, the whisper is annoying, but it's a far cry from the cacophony of condemnation that once filled my head. Time is not the only reason for this dampening, as I've found that the voice and its noise grow fainter the longer I am able to keep my feet planted on the ground beneath me. The longer I maintain my sobriety and the relationships that sustain and support me, and the greater my capacity for renegotiation, re-evaluation, and recalibration grows, the fainter that voice becomes. It's a slow process, but one that has allowed me to take some pretty big steps in recent years.

My campaign of change extended beyond my use of narcotics and booze to my lifestyle as well. When I'd managed to break free from the restrictive chains of substances, I set my sights on eliminating yet another item from my roster of consumption: meat. Actually, to be honest, I sought to eliminate all animal products, but simply saying "meat" felt more impactful and dramatic (some habits die hard, what can I say?). In any case, veganism was the next horizon I became determined to conquer, mostly because adopting this diet just made sense to me. I had learned how to love and show compassion to myself. Thus, it stood to reason that the care that started with me should be extended to those beyond me. With any luck, I would be able to extend this compassion so that it becomes part of every aspect of my life—so that I can feel and share it as much as humanly possible. As with so many stories of someone's transition to a vegan lifestyle, you may be reading this expecting me to begin some sort of sales pitch convincing you to rush to the store and buy a lifetime's worth of non-dairy milk alternatives. Rest assured that that sales pitch isn't coming. (Also, please don't buy so much milk—you'll never use it all before it goes bad.)

While I certainly hope that there are aspects of my story you can take and use to learn or change something in your life, the entire idea behind me telling you all this is so that you understand what change really entails, assuming that you don't already know. For you to alter anything in your life, and for you to do so radically with your eye on permanent amendment, there must first exist a concerted, comprehensive effort. I made these changes because they were what I needed in order to improve my life and begin working toward the future I wanted. Whatever you tackle in your life will be vastly different. That's precisely the point, and it's precisely your task as well. In order to improve your own situation, you first have to find what needs mending. Once that's been identified, you have to ask yourself whether you're looking for a deep, permanent change or something more temporary. With that question answered, you can begin to build the habits, actions, and internal shifts that will help you access the new-and-improved version of your life, the version you deserve.

# The Doctoral Journey

Years ago, when I obtained my MFA, a small part of me knew that I would return to academia as a student at one point or another. A lot of time had passed since my graduation at 27, but still, my conviction remained as strong as ever despite the many setbacks and exhibitions of ill judgment that had delayed this particular aspiration. However, as harsh as the derailment brought on by some of these events was, that conviction never faded, and I was reminded time and time again of my desire to pursue this degree. It's intriguing, I think, that I held on to this dream for as long as I did, given that it didn't cross my mind every day. It was only in those moments when my mind was clear enough and I could sort of ground myself that I was able to understand what I really, truly desired and how those wants aligned with the things I needed to flourish. It was in those same moments that I once again felt that unquenchable thirst and love for lifelong learning. Moreover, those instances also allowed me to see that this degree represented the ultimate peak of achievement that people like me weren't supposed to reach.

It may seem inconsequential or uninteresting, the fact that an idea I once had about pursuing a doctoral degree would stay lodged in my brain for that long. The thing you have to understand is that, on any given day, a myriad of other thoughts, feelings, and desires will race through my mind. Mostly, these are singular occurrences, and many of the things that pop up will pass me by. However, it's rare for something to stick, much less for it to transform into a genuine desire, and even rarer for that same desire to resonate with something deep inside me, striking a spark that begins to fizzle in my soul. This idea did, and it affected me in a way that very few things do. Every time I try to describe the feeling to someone, I find that it becomes more and more difficult. While I can't exactly describe what it is, I can tell you that this feeling is the same one that arises when I think about performing. It's the same feeling that keeps pulling me back to acting time and time again. Also, it's the same feeling that pulled me back to idea of doing a third degree on more than one occasion.

I do think that, perhaps, my motivation to pursue this degree was also born out of an unconscious desire to prove that not only could I do great things, but I could also be a great person. I was the only person to whom this would be proven, but I suppose it's still something part of me felt had to be done to fully recover and heal from my past. Whatever the reason for it, I felt like I couldn't rest until it was done. It was like a deep, profound thirst that would set up camp in my head, interfering with nearly everything else until it was slaked. It did occur to me, as it may have occurred to some of you now, that chasing the fulfillment of this desire was in some ways just a substitution for the process of seeking out, procuring, and using substances. While I can certainly understand why you might see it that way, this particular yen was different from the others. When I was using, I would just blindly accept whatever it was I had to do to get my fix. This time around, I was purposefully embracing the drive I felt to see this through, and more importantly, I was heading into all of it with a clear head.

I'm sure that you can call this an impulse of sorts, but it's one that I would argue is perfectly fine to give in to, even if it means getting hurt again or failing somehow. As it turns out, failure was something I would become reacquainted with very, very soon. While I did end up with my doctoral degree, it took me several tries to get here. The first attempt, a degree in the field of Organizational Leadership, lasted just a little over a year, with my studies being interrupted by an announcement from the department that they would be "teaching out" the program in which I had enrolled. This was the result of the Chair of the program's several-months-long research project examining how employable those who held this degree were. As it turns out, the answer was not very much. Subsequently, the course would no longer be presented due to the findings of the Chair's cost-benefit initiative. We were informed that given the lack of employability with which this degree would provide us, even within academia, our cohort would be the last.

As you may have expected, this news enraged me. I felt robbed, particularly as I had only just begun to use the part of my brain where logic was held, which had for so long been subdued under the weight of drugs, alcohol, and emotional fluctuations. Everything I had anticipated would come to pass with this program was erased within minutes. As luck would have it, my newfound sense of self-efficacy and significantly higher levels of self-love had endowed me with the ability to (occasionally) speak up for myself. I demanded answers about the program's cancellation, and about the sudden delivery of these results. I saw no reason why they couldn't have conducted the study much earlier, thus sparing us all a lot of time and effort. It may shock you to hear that I never did get answers to my questions. To be fair, it wasn't exactly like I stuck around to hear their response, either.

Whatever issues I voiced regarding the premature end of the program fell on deaf ears, and I decided to withdraw from the doctoral program. I recall the difficulty that went into making that final move. It didn't matter that the course was dead in the water. I had set my sights on making a reality of that dream I had carried with me for so long, and now found myself back at square one. For the time being, there was nothing to do but carry on and wait for the next opportunity to present itself. As angry as I was at the department head and all those involved in shutting the program down, I had to admit that my studies coming to an end had a silver lining, however thin it may have been. I now had time to take a step back and take another look at what it was I wanted to learn, as well as how I'd go about it. I was determined to see this degree through, but was worried that the same thing would happen if I just picked the next-best program. With the time afforded to me by the silver lining, I could vet programs thoroughly, assess the pros and cons, and make a well-informed decision for my second try. I did all of this with a number of courses, and finally ended up enrolling in a PhD program that was conducted entirely online. This time, the field was management, and I saw no way in which this degree could make me anything but employable. A manager is always needed, right? So off I went to doctoral degree attempt number two.

Regrettably, this round resulted in a similar (if slightly less out-of-the blue) K.O. I once again decided to suspend my participation in the program. Before your mind jumps to something horrible like a relapse or a surprise prison sentence, the determining factor was time. No sooner had I enrolled and read through the course syllabi than it became glaringly apparent that there was way too much to do, and entirely too little time to do it in. Over the course of the program, every week would come with about 200 pages of reading, with a new paper rounding out each weekly rota. You remember that self-awareness I'd gained since working the steps?

Well, it was that same sense of perception that let me know I was in no way cut out for this. The other program I had enrolled in had averaged about 100 pages of reading per week, if it was that much, and I'd barely managed to complete all of it on time. Truth be told, the voice of self-awareness that was dissuading me from doing all this turned out to be the voice of self-doubt. I'm not sure if the two are conflated in other peoples' minds, but in mine their timbres are entirely too similar, leading to some nasty tricks being played. In this instance, the trick was over quickly, and my sense of self-doubt came rushing to the front almost immediately after my first glance at the workload. It assured me, in the slimiest of its voices, that I simply didn't have the capacity to do anything close to this much work. My efforts were insignificant and always would be, so there was absolutely no reason at all for me to even attempt doing something that so obviously wasn't meant for me.

The irony is, I was right. At least, my brain was right about not sticking with things that aren't suited to me. That online program wasn't for me—not because of my abilities, but simply because what it would teach me and what I hoped to achieve simply didn't align. Besides, I could easily read 200 pages of textbook material every week, perhaps even more if I were pushed. Had I done it before? No. Was I still convinced it was well within my abilities? Yes, if only because it wasn't nearly as impossible as I had initially thought. People had done it in the past.

Hell, people were doing it as I was debating whether it could be done. Even if I wasn't one of those people yet, I would have to become one if I ever hoped of realizing this dream of mine. However, there was no way I would just *do it*. No, this time around I had to make sure that everything was just right, from the course content to the compulsory reading to the program itself. I recall this time in my life as being one in which it felt like emotional dominoes were falling, one after the other. First came the realization that completing a doctoral degree was something I was more than capable of doing. Then came the commitment to actually seeing it through. Finally, the last domino to fall was a promise I made to myself, vowing that I wouldn't even think of enrolling at another institution if I wasn't entirely, 1,000% sure that nothing would stand in the way of me donning that cap and gown for the third time.

My determination was resolute, and my will was iron. I was so determined to have things work out this time that another year had passed, three in total since I first re-entered the world of tertiary education, before I found the program I was looking for. My search led me down more avenues than you could possibly imagine. I weighed different courses against one another, looked at employment rates, the availability of jobs, examined future outlook data, and asked a thousand questions.

The process was long and tedious, but I eventually began to find some of the answers I was looking for. In the process, I made use of a number of tools to help me find the program that would fit me like a glove. One of these tools helped me determine which fields of study would prove most beneficial to me by helping me to identify everything I have either loved or felt some sort of affinity toward. Ultimately, the goal was to discover what your life's passion and purpose were. The tool did this by showing you some of the themes present in your life. Mine were fairly obvious and included the fact that I love people and studying their behaviors. This came as a surprise to me when it was first revealed. And yet, as I looked back to my younger years, it seemed to make much more sense than I thought it would. I had always been studying people, even if I wasn't aware of it at the time. As a child, my choice to play Jezebel in my brother's and my domestic theater stretched beyond merely wanting to dress up and act in a way that more closely emulated the feminine energy to which I was so strongly drawn. Instead, I wanted to understand why different people assume the different behaviors they do. This analysis of mankind was what got me into trouble when I was young and regularly attempted to hug strangers. To my young mind, and even to its adult version, the next best thing after hugging a random person is getting to know them, as this was an embrace of its own, and the first step toward accepting someone as they are. In hindsight, I did for others what I hoped someone would someday do for me.

As the old adage goes, the third time was the charm. And the charm saw me move away from the strictly business-oriented degrees I'd pursued before, this time opting to study a doctorate of psychology (or PsyD, as you may know it) in business psychology. I remember making the decision to enroll in this program, and how much easier and more natural it felt than either of the times before. Everything I read about the program made me feel grounded and did wonders for my confidence in my abilities, as well. The further I explored this topic, the stronger I began to feel the sense of peace and conviction that I had lost so long ago. Most important of all, this return occurred all of its own accord. I wasn't pushing to feel these things, nor did I feel compelled to pretend as though I did. It was all very natural, further underscoring just how perfect this degree was for me. Naturally, I gravitated toward this offering for other reasons, as well. Somewhere in my adult life, I had developed an interest in business and how it was conducted on both the large and small scale. Moreover, my lived experiences left me with a sense of disregard (maybe even outright disdain) for things like profits and capitalism. However, what I was most interested in exploring was that space where the life we lead in the workplace overlaps with the person we are outside the office, resulting in a sort of extension of our self-worth and overall well-being forming in the professional spaces we inhabit.

All in all, there was no end to what I wanted to learn, and I was eager to jump in. Of course, as has been the case for the majority of things in my life, challenges were never too far behind, and they started manifesting not long after my enrollment in the PsyD program. In the past, these obstacles would likely have tripped me up before my journey had properly begun. However, this was my third foray into the world of the doctoral degree, and I was equipped with a steel-like conviction and the determination to work as hard and fast as I could. I was willing to do whatever it took to ensure that I reached the finish line.

In the end, this involved cutting down on my work hours and moving back in with my parents, though these sacrifices were trifles when compared to what I stood to gain. My motivation came partially from the realization that I had been enjoying various forms of privilege for a solid portion of my life, even in those years when I buried myself under bottles and substances. In the past, whenever the types of challenges I faced during the program would arise, I would cling to my privilege for as long as I could. But a lot had changed since then, and I intended only to make use of it for as long as I needed. To me, this was a crucial distinction. I was still privileged, but I was no longer dependent.

And so, close to four years after I took the first steps down the road, my doctoral journey came to an end. I had my fair share of setbacks, but still managed to graduate, first of my cohort, with a GPA of 4.0. It's essential to note that I don't share this with you in the hopes of attracting compliments, praise, or validation. Rather, I not only want to demonstrate just how far I've come since those first party-filled days, but also wish to share a story with you about my time in this program.

The course I had enrolled in was constructed in hybrid form, meaning that the majority of my reading and research took place at home, with a few trips to the campus in Chicago rounding out the learning experience. It was during one of my days in the Windy City that I ran into the school's assistant dean. More accurately, she stopped me as we were walking past each other. We had never met before, and the only reason she approached me in the first place was to offer her congratulations to me for having achieved such a high grade-point average. At the time, the encounter was nice enough, and it was only in the weeks following it that I would realize that we had never met before. Her stopping me meant she knew who I was and had intentionally decided to reach out. But the encounter itself isn't the most remarkable part of the story. It's what she said that really stuck with me. After she congratulated me, I said (in all sincerity) something to the effect of "Oh, well, I'm sure just about everyone here has a 4.0." To this day, her response remains stuck in my mind. My reply took her slightly aback, and as an answer she said: "That's interesting you would say that, and I wonder what is informing you to feel that way. You see, it's actually rare in this department to graduate with a 4.0. So, what do you think this says about you?" Admittedly, this was a very "psychologist" answer to give, even more so if you consider the fact that she said it while wearing a genuine smile. Regardless of its nature, her response was one of the most profound things I had ever heard. Upon reflection, I think that what it says about me is that I finally found my corner of the sky, a corner where (miraculously) I've managed to build my own church, and find my own form of sacred, secular religion. Additionally, what it says is that, even in the face of great achievement, that little voice that sows doubt and disapproval will still make itself heard, even if its words don't always make it through to my consciousness.

## Telling Stories to Help Others

If you recall, storytelling has long been one of my greatest passions. Though I'm not sure how, I'm pretty confident that my stint as Jezebel will go down in history. The opportunities to regale others grew fewer and further between as the years went on, but still my passion remained. This takes us back awhile, to the middle of time studying for my Master's degree. As part of the program, I was tasked with creating a thesis film, a project I had decided to title *The Poser: Being Anyone but Yourself*. In case it wasn't apparent, the main character in the film was me, albeit a version with a twist. I have long since found myself empathetic to the cause of transgender individuals who populate the queer community right alongside me. When the opportunity for some artistic flexibility and expression made itself known, I decided to run with it and created the character of Paul, who is assigned female at birth, but who transitions in young adulthood. The film followed Paul as he desperately tries to conceal the truth of his identity so that he might be accepted by the world. I felt that telling Paul's story was an opportunity for me to comment on the privilege I enjoyed. While I worked hard as a child to hide my more effeminate side, it was no longer something I was concerned with. Both the internal and external difficulties I had largely disappeared—at least as they related to my sexuality as part of my identity. This was not the case for members of the trans community, nor for those who identify as anything else but cisgender. In fact, this has only become worse as time has gone by, with Black trans youth becoming especially vulnerable.

Because the experience of transgender people is different from my own, and because I can't presume to understand the trans experience in the same way, I decided to focus on the things that my journey would have in common with that of the character of Paul. Little did I know that, by the time principal photography rolled around, there would be an actual trans woman on set acting in one of the other roles, let alone one who would soon make great strides in her career. I digress and must confess that I became exponentially more nervous about Paul's character after learning about the actress's identity. I so desperately wanted to provide this person and his story with a feeling of justice and hoped that it would translate to viewers, especially those who were part of the trans community themselves. My nerves were also stoked in part because I hoped to make this a through-line in my work—telling stories that could help people and communities connect with one another, especially those who have experienced marginalization and oppression, both past and present.

A few years later, when I was completing my doctoral studies, this line of inquiry and creation would continue with the story of a trans person who was in the process of transitioning, and how it affected the professional aspects of their life. Through this experience, it became clear to me that when organizations allow their members and employees to transform themselves on any level they wish, the institutional body as a whole will benefit and may even experience some positive transformation itself. This is especially true when support is given to those for whom making such changes has historically been much more difficult.

After this, I made another short film. Forming part of the work I did for my thesis, the film was named *Being Transgressive*, and it worked as a form of entertainment-education to lay the groundwork for addressing training videos that fully emerge the audience into a storyline with an embedded message for change. This method is well-established, having been around for about 40 years by the time I made use of it, and has produced great effects in both local productions as well as mass-media projects. I was well aware of the fact that my work would by no means solve the issues that so many people face, but even such a small contribution could help bring the matter to more people's attention, which is a small victory in itself. It was victory for me on a personal level, as well, as it provided me with another opportunity to put my skills, knowledge, and passion to use so that I may do what I love best.

As the years have gone on, I've had some time to reflect on my experiences with performance and its related forms of art. In doing so, I've come to understand that every chance I have been given to embody a character and tell their story has meant so much more to me, and has made a much deeper impact, than simple entertainment. As I continue to engage with this medium, I increasingly feel that the very best stories are those that make their viewers think deeply and seriously about a topic. They are the stories that leave people with a desire to not only contemplate their own decisions in life, but also to improve them. I know that telling these types of stories is more than possible, and it's exactly what I hope to be a part of for the rest of my life. I suspect that it's led to both of our presences within the pages of this book, as well. I suppose that this book is a kind of full-circle occurrence, with my burning desire to share the things I have learned leading to its creation.

Crucially, it's this desire that has compelled me to share so much of my story with you. I don't want to garner your sympathy or pity. Instead, I hope that telling you all these things will lead to understanding, hope, empathy, and encouragement. Making it through the darkest days of your life absolutely calls for celebration, and coming together in this way is just one of the many means we have to create some beauty amongst all the ugliness of the world.

# The Future

In recent years, there have been some studies performed in the field of quantitative ratios, particularly regarding how we can put them to use as a way of trying to elicit optimism. The result of this research points to an average ratio of 1:3, though ratios can go up to as high as 1:7. Research experts on optimism understand this range to be the need people demonstrate to counteract each negative thought or experience they have with between 3 and 7 positive thoughts or behaviors. If this sliding scale of ratios is indicative of anything, it's that the negativity in our lives has the potential to become pretty powerful. This isn't to say that negativity doesn't have a part to play, or that our lives should be entirely devoid of anything less than 100% positivity. What the potential power of bad things actually means is that we should deal with these less-than-ideal things head on. Moreover, it means that positivity doesn't just happen, but instead requires real, intentional effort in order to counterbalance the effects of what has come from the unpleasant side of the universe.

I know it may seem confusing or intimidating, perhaps even strange to see emotions and experiences through a lens constructed of numbers and mathematical ratios. However, for someone like me, approaching things from this point of view has proved to be incredibly helpful. It's enabled me to put my life into perspective. For all the bad things that have happened in my life, and that will potentially happen in the time to come (although with a little less intensely this time around, I hope), there was and still is a great deal of work for me to do. This "work," for want of a better term, is largely for my own benefit as it involves constantly learning how I can make myself and the pieces in my life better, and it's likely that I'll continue this process until I die. But the thing is, I'm not dead...yet, and until that day does roll around, I will do my absolute best at being the healthiest, most awkward, emotional, experimental, and loving creature I can be. And that's something that no person, no thing, and no experience can take away from me.

# Chapter 8:

# I'm Not Dead...Yet

Many events and phases in my life have come to an end, but of all the journeys that have finished, this is perhaps the most bittersweet. On the one hand, I'm happy that my story has progressed to this point because it means I can share with you all that I have learned in my many, many deeds. On the other, however, I'm not sure I'm quite ready to put all this behind me. While I have absolutely no desire to live in the past, and while I have worked to move past so much of what happened, I think this will be a different kind of conclusion. And after all this time, it'll finally be a happy one.

## Taking Stock

Over the course of my life, the things I've seen and experienced have left me with what I like to think of as emotional souvenirs. Each of these curios has become something that I try to incorporate into my life on a daily basis. Now, admittedly, these are all things I've gleaned from my own life, so they might not work for everyone. But that's precisely what I love about the human experience—though we're all similar in some pretty fundamental ways, not everything will work for everyone—at least, not in exact the same way. I think this applies to my parents especially, odd as it may seem. They raised both my brother and me under the umbrella of the same organized religion they adhere to, and yet I found that the same system of beliefs they clung to so tightly became suffocating when applied to my life and my personhood. Moral of the story? There's something out there for everyone. Crucially, the disparity between your values and beliefs and those of other people is not, under any circumstances, license to disparage or judge those who differ from you. In my opinion, this is where so many people and institutions go wrong. While it's certainly understandable that people would like to share the things they believe in and hold close to their own heart, ostensibly under the guise of helping others adopt the same tools and coping skills, attempting proselytizing on a mass scale is not the way to go. Nor is the rejection and condemnation of those who have no desire to adopt your beliefs, or who would prefer to stick to the practices they've already incorporated into their lives.

Though those emotional souvenirs have been combined to form some sort of coping system, they are far from the only thing I turn to for support. As evidenced by the passion and deep, deep investment I felt throughout the entirety of my doctoral program, I had decided to adopt the science of psychology as my new religion. To be perfectly honest, I doubt that the term "religion" is apt for what I found within this world. Instead of replacing the tenets of the Jehovah's Witnesses with something else, I found an alignment in which passions, interests, purpose, and sense of spirituality all connected with one another. In psychology, I discovered a range of models and frameworks I could use to understand how people change and flourish, and how these things can become sustainable in the long run. Not to get too technical, or to reveal too many of my true, nerdy colors, but there are two models that influenced me and changed my view of the world more profoundly than any of the others I studied. The theories in question are the transtheoretical model of behavior change, as well as something called PERMA (an acronym for positive emotion, engagement, positive relationships, meaning, and achievement). The thoughts and feelings I have about these models could fill the pages of another manuscript, so we'll leave them to be seen here in name alone. Ultimately, all this comes down to the profundity I found in books, texts, and research, and that I continue to rediscover time and time again, just like that time I opened up my first acting book back in New York City.

Of course, we can't discuss what I've gained from my educational experiences without mentioning one of my first loves: performing. In the time I spent studying acting, I learned something that I still, to this day, connect to the concept of flourishing. Because there are so many different schools of thought, models, frameworks, tools, and concepts tied to the field, it can be all too easy to become overwhelmed by the sheer number of options presented to those who are just starting out. Consequently, it becomes incredibly important to sift through all of this to find what works for you on an individual level, adopting that which serves you and disposing of that which does not. This practice may be difficult, however, as it requires consistent, concerted effort, coupled with the determination to keep learning by doing, as well as accepting the fact that the learning experience lends itself to failure. Whenever things don't work out as we had planned, it's up to us to continue the process and try again with something new.

These are all ideas I attempt to maintain as the main, guiding aspects in my life. For me, exploration is one of the greatest privileges I enjoy, and I try to do it as much as possible. Should this process uncover something that serves me and enforces the values I hold, I try my best to ensure that it remains in my life for as long as possible. Moreover, I try to keep in mind that there was a period in my life when I never thought sobriety would be possible for me, that I would never be able to change my lifestyle to become healthier, and during which I was convinced that I would never again enjoy a relationship with any kind of genuine connection. To my surprise, all of this proved to be within my reach. When it comes down to it, change is never impossible, no matter how dire the circumstances may be. People can and do change, but the first step toward making any sort of lasting amendments to our lives is looking inward, finding what's important to us, and building a relationship with ourselves to serve as the foundation for all that is to come.

## Being Mindful

By this point, there should be very little that comes as a surprise, especially when it comes to things I've picked up over the years. I think we've been through enough together to have deduced that, if there's one thing I love, it's learning something new. With this in mind, we go back to the time of my doctoral degree once more. This time, we remain in the world of psychology, but turn our minds away from the world of business to instead focus on more holistic forms of mental well-being. Yes, indeed, one more practice I adopted into my life is that of mindfulness. As with the psychological models I found myself drawn to, I could write volumes about the mindfulness concepts that interest me. Fortunately, this has been done by many other, more qualified practitioners. What remains is for me to share with you the practices I tried out and found to be beneficial.

Mindfulness, even in its simplest form, has always appealed to me. For the longest time, analyzing and interpreting the things and people that surround me has been one of my favorite pastimes. You can imagine my joy when I discovered mindfulness and its foundational practice of situational and contextual awareness. However, whatever love I had developed for the practice was immediately deepened and solidified by the idea that this awareness cannot operate in isolation and should instead be employed alongside a nonjudgmental sensibility. As I'm sure you know, my life has been characterized by judgment, often manifesting in extreme ways at either the positive or negative end of the spectrum. As a result, practicing this type of awareness while keeping my mind stable in a state of neutrality was more difficult than I imagined. But, then, I've never been one to shy away from a challenge. Once I got into the swing of things, mindfulness practices ended up being more beneficial to my life than I had anticipated, with the breathing and meditation exercises I employ proving to be especially useful in those moments when my mind once again becomes too harsh on itself, or I find my heartbeat quickening with anxiety when thinking about the future. There are very few instances in which I have to be reminded about the gift that is life, but when my awareness and appreciation does slip a bit, I know I can simply turn to mindfulness to help get my mindset back into place. These dips aren't pleasant, but they are part of being human, something I'm still working on accepting.

## Accepting What Is

I've written a lot about acceptance and the processes that have led me to making peace with parts of my life. And while I certainly hope that my experiences haven't come across as easy or inconsequential, getting over this particular hurdle was one of the more difficult things I've had to do in my lifetime. Truth be told, all the convictions I made, the lessons I learned, and the practices I integrated into my life did bring about the change I was hoping they would. But for all their power, time still proved to be the greatest force of healing I have ever known. Accepting things as they are is, as I'm sure you can imagine, a hard thing to do. This is especially true when you look back at your past and wish that the majority of your actions and decisions could either be amended or erased. Of course, this isn't possible, and the only recourse is to find a way to live with what's happened. In part, I've achieved this through each of the techniques and models we've already explored. Meditating regularly and viewing my life in a different way have certainly helped, if only by allowing my mind with the space and power it needed to make sense of everything that has come to pass.

In the end, what makes acceptance possible is not only time, but also space. The further your growth continues, the further away you move from each of those moments in life that, if I'm being totally honest, I sometimes wish hadn't happened. It's only once this space has been gained that you come to understand that, as wonderful as the prospect of that aforementioned erasure would be, everything that happened was, in fact, necessary to my development as a person. This is a crucial realization, one that has helped me comprehend the fact that just because I accept something, that doesn't mean I cannot change it—or maybe even just attempt to do so.

Now this doesn't mean that I'm not regretful about some of the decisions I made, as those resultant behaviors did inflict pain and suffering on some of the people I love the most. However, enough time has passed for me to comprehend the fact that everything that happened, happened. I know this tautology sounds like one of those platitudes that people often pull out and present as a legitimate concept in the absence of any real, concrete wisdom. Rest assured that this isn't that. Rather, it's the comprehension that all of the wishing in the world wouldn't provide me with the ability to traverse time and undo some of my decisions, prevent some of my actions, or put the past version of myself on a path that would ultimately join up with another road entirely—at least not until someone makes a real DeLorean and we can all go back to the future.

With the benefit of time and space (sometimes referred to colloquially as "hindsight"), I have been able to make my peace with the past, particularly with my inability to remedy any of the hurt I caused. Note that I mean the pain that existed in that moment. The hurt (and the effects) that has lived on throughout the years—I am more than capable of working to ameliorate that. Additionally, with this hindsight, healing can only take place once I accept the truth of the person I was back then and the truth of the decisions he made. It's something that hasn't come to me easily, mostly because there are undeniably parts of my past I would prefer to forget for the rest of my natural life. Unfortunately (or fortunately, maybe), life doesn't work that way, and I will have to reckon with who I was and what I did every day I remain on this Earthly plane. Believe me when I say that this process is sometimes very painful, but the results will make it more than worth the effort.

## This Life Is Beautiful

Acceptance is a process, and at the same time, it's only the first step in a larger progression of actions and amendments that steadily come together to facilitate healing. In its capacity as a step, acceptance acts as a catalyst for realization. In my case, learning to make my peace with the past and reconcile the truth of its existence as part of my life meant simultaneously realizing that, when all is said and done, my life is worth living. Not only worth living, but also worth celebrating and embracing to the fullest extent possible. This realization was quite profound and changed the way I look at myself and the way I approach my life as a whole. Interestingly, and wonderfully, this profundity stretched beyond myself and allowed me to gain the same level of appreciation for the lives and loves of the people, places, and things I am surrounded with on a daily basis.

In terms of practical implementation, this newfound appreciation for all things life-related manifested as a conscious decision to enjoy more of what I saw, felt, heard, and experienced. Cliché as it might sound, it meant making an effort to avoid taking things for granted. We walk in front of the same landscaping each day, and each day there is something we have yet to notice in what we repeatedly see. We need to take the time to acknowledge them, as they were always there, just waiting to be noticed by us. This newness, if you will, and the sense of awe found in what was previously mundane and unappreciated is amazingly beautiful to experience.

# Being Naked and Unafraid

Writing this book and telling my story has been something I debated doing for years. And when it finally came time to do it, I can't describe the experience as anything other than feeling naked. It was a process I had started years ago, then stopped, and started again before stopping. Obviously, the stopping didn't stick, so here we are. That being said, the staccato pattern of my attempts has largely been psychological in nature. I was afraid of reliving the things I'd been through and the things I'd done. At that time, I didn't have nearly as much peace as I do now, and it felt to me as though revisiting and recontextualizing the events from my past would be the same as regressing to the person I was when they took place. Even in the moments when my concern wasn't for something so severe, I was still hesitant, held back by feelings of worry that I would unnecessarily be reopening old wounds that had only very recently begun to show signs of healing. These thoughts would spin around my head on a loop whenever I tried to put pen to paper. So, I waited until they became a bit quieter before trying again.

Finally, when I returned to the project for the last time (read: this time), I understood that it had to be like so many other things in my life. If I didn't deal with it, if I didn't make an attempt to reconcile the present version of me with the one that existed in decades gone by, then everything attached to my past would simply keep reappearing in my life until I either made another move to solve my problems or, alternatively, until I died. All things considered, these options didn't really seem to be all that conducive to the healing I was trying to undergo, so I instead turned to that old, dependable practice of mine: storytelling. This time around, however, there were no Biblical characters, fairytale crickets, or prison production clergymen to hide behind. In this instance, telling my story meant doing it as myself, and doing it unabashedly at that. It's a bit like coming out of the womb as I release myself from the wounds of the past, thus becoming authentic and naked, exposed for all the world to see. And though this catharsis is mine, I hope you create your own, because you deserve it. All of us do.

# Conclusion

I look back on so much of my journey and find myself reminiscing in wonderment, slightly baffled at the sheer number of things I've been through in my time on this Earth. Though I'm not a betting man, I'd wager that the average person shouldn't ever have to live through so much turmoil in order to better themselves—I'd wager that this shouldn't happen to anyone at all. And yet, each of those experiences was something I needed to have happen. I don't think this makes me remarkable or sets me aside from the rest of the world in any way.

After all, everyone has their own story, their own history, and their own times of chaos, pain, and difficulty. Difficult as it may be to reconcile experiences like these with belief in the plan of a higher power, I still do believe that every person on Earth was put here for a reason. I don't think this makes me religious, but I'd like to think that it does make me a believer, especially in the power of the human spirit.

Additionally, what it makes me is one among many, many who have suffered in one way or another. I believe this unites me with a great many people. In the same way, I feel connected to other queer people, other Latinos, Americans, people living with HIV, those who struggle with substance use, people who have survived sexual abuse, who have survived cancer, and who are surviving whatever it is that the universe is throwing at them.

Having experiences like these can be isolating sometimes, for a number of reasons. But if there is one thing I hope that you will take with you now that our journey together has come to an end, it's this: You are not alone. You never have been, and I promise you never will be.

# References

de Boer, C. (1978). The polls: Attitudes toward homosexuality. *Public Opinion Quarterly*, 42(2), 265. https://doi.org/10.1086/268448

Kruhly, M. (2012, July 17). What America looked like: Puerto Rican slums in the early 1970s. *The Atlantic*. https://www.theatlantic.com/national/archive/2012/07/what-america-looked-like-puerto-rican-slums-in-the-early-1970s/259878/

www.ingramcontent.com/pod-product-compliance
Lightning Source LLC
Chambersburg PA
CBHW020225130626
46549CB00005B/1751